A STEP-BY-STEP GUIDE TO EMBROIDERY

*Through the Seasons*

# PAINT WITH THREAD

## EMILLIE FERRIS

DAVID & CHARLES

www.davidandcharles.com

# CONTENTS

# WELCOME

Oh hello there, kindred spirit. I'm beyond honoured that you chose my book – thank you. By picking it up and reading these words from wherever you are, we are now connected in some way, which is rather beautiful. This is *our* book.

## WHAT WILL YOU LEARN?

In this book, I show you how to embroider realistic images, even if you've never picked up a needle before. You will gain confidence in your abilities, and hopefully go on to create your own designs in the future. I'll introduce you to all the materials you need and teach you how to transfer the pattern onto fabric. We will delve into how to use Long-and-Short Stitch to create flowing stitch directions - ideal for embroidering the featured flora and fauna.

Whatever your current embroidery experience and knowledge, I'm sure you will enjoy embroidering the following projects and learn something new along the way.

## WHO IS THIS BOOK FOR?

This book is suitable for all skill levels, absolute beginners and seasoned stitchers alike, so be welcome my stitching friends!

You are more capable than you may think you are – sometimes we just need someone to explain it to us first. In older times, the only people I would have been able to share my knowledge with would have been with my family, passed down through the generations. Thankfully we now have books, and the internet. I'm beyond grateful that I get to show you the way I like to embroider. With this in mind, I have tried to explain everything just as I would when explaining to a dear friend. Embroidery is an art form that feels like home – allow me to welcome you into my humble abode, everyone is welcome here.

## PAINTING WITH THREAD

All the projects in this book use my preferred methods, tried and tested continuously by me since 2013. The embroidery technique I use is referred to as needle-painting, though you may also know this method as Long-and-Short Stitch, thread painting or silk shading. It is essentially a very free and non-restrictive way to embroider. Ideal for filling large surface areas of fabric, it is essentially like painting on a canvas, but rather than using paint, you are using thread.

I use needle-painting in all my embroideries – it is perfect for stitching natural, organic forms. In the very beginning, I unknowingly taught myself this method through joyful experimentation. After a few years, I acquired the knowledge that I was actually using the technique of Long-and-Short Stitch. There are hundreds of different embroidery stitches in existence, but I don't believe you need to learn them all to enjoy the art of embroidery and see your creative vision come to life. In its most basic form, I predominately use a simple straight stitch over and over again. I just change the stitch length, direction and colour to suit my design.

## YOU ARE AN ARTIST

*"And suddenly you know: it's time to start something new and trust the magic of beginnings."*

**Meister Eckhart, philosopher, mystic and theologian**

I know it can be intimidating starting a new project, especially more so if this is an entirely new world to you. Hence why I'll be holding your hand every step of the way with detailed step-by-step instructions. Once you've completed your first embroidery, your confidence and sense of satisfaction will give you the boost you need. If you are a beginner, I recommend embroidering the dandelion first as it takes the least amount of time to complete. With embroidery, the battle can often be a lack of patience, rather than a lack of skill. Once you get into the flow and find your joy in it, you won't want to stop embroidering.

8

Help yourself on your endeavour by gathering the materials you need, which is always a good place to start. Then when inspiration strikes and you want to try a project from the book, you have no excuses or barriers – your hoop, needle and thread will be ready, patiently waiting for you. Set yourself up for success. Let a friend or family member know you want to try embroidery and set an evening aside to try it together.

I have created all the patterns in this book with clear colour guides and instructions, but please know that you are encouraged to add your own personal touch. There are no rules here. If you feel more comfortable using a different technique, or want to use more than one strand of floss at a time, please do so. You don't even have to keep your embroidery in the hoop if that's not your style – instead, embroider any of these patterns onto your jeans, jackets, shirts, bags, rucksack, cushions, hats or whatever else takes your fancy!

There is only one you in the entire world, who has experienced life the way you have, your influences, your creativity – you are one of a kind! Just because I embroider one way, it doesn't mean you have to limit yourself to my preferred techniques. Trust yourself, you are human, therefore you are an artist.

## TAKE YOUR TIME

Let's get one thing straight – embroidery is seriously cool. I've created this book because I want to encourage as many people as possible to pick up an embroidery needle. In a digital age where everything is instantaneous, it's important to take the time to create something with your own two hands. Embroidering encourages you to sit down, breath and ease into an evening (or a whole day!) of creativity and relaxation. The repetitive nature makes it a great way to switch off from the outside world and become wholly engrossed in creating something. I hope you fall in love with the ancient art of embroidery and show the world how great something can be if you simply take the time to create it.

If you share photos of your work online, please tag my Instagram handle @emillieferris or use the hashtag #patternsbyemillie.

# LET ME INTRODUCE MYSELF...

Hi! My name's Emillie. I'm an artist living and working in Warwickshire, England, and love to honour nature and other beloved treasures through the process of hand-embroidery. Growing up in the countryside allowed me to see the landscapes change with the seasons, which in turn fuelled a fascination for wildlife, British folklore and natural history. Since starting my embroidery journey in 2013, I have worked with a variety of clients the world over, most of whom commission me to produce my extremely detailed and bespoke embroidered pet portraits. By 2018, I had decided to share my self-taught knowledge and passion for embroidery with others. These days, I concentrate on teaching through digital tutorials and kits, alongside selling pins and other original artwork.

## A PASSION FOR EMBROIDERY

*"The past is not dead, it is living in us, and will be alive in the future which we are now helping to make."*

**William Morris**

Due to its timeless nature, embroidery makes me feel connected to the past and all of the other people in history that took up this art form. It roots me to the present moment, and is a great way to switch off from the digital world. Using your hands to create something that you're proud of is a feeling everyone deserves to experience. In a modern society, we have incredible new media technologies, such as virtual art, computer animation, digital art and so on, all of which are credible and inspiring art forms that gift us with films and video games. However, we can find balance by creating something from a few humble materials. It just feels right to physically use your body and hold the creation in your hands. The time and parts of yourself you put into it – that's wholesome, that's life.

It's also great fun to challenge yourself by emulating realism in embroidery. It often surprises people when they learn my creations are hand embroidered. With paint, you can blend any colour you desire; however, I enjoy the challenge of embroidering my subject matter with a limited colour palette. You can create the illusion of a certain colour from afar by blending two or three different colours. The texture of the thread also works well when trying to emulate the fur on animals, or the fluffy body of a moth. All of this suits my style as I'm always inspired by the magic of the natural world.

Painting with thread gives me the freedom to create art just as I would when drawing or painting with watercolours. Embroidery will always be my most beloved and favourite art form. It engenders a feeling of contentment and well-being. There is an atmosphere of coziness and comfortable conviviality. When I'm embroidering, I belong, I am home.

# TOOLS & MATERIALS

First let's gather the tools and materials needed – there aren't many, but each one has a crucial role to play! The bonus is that they all look so pretty too, adding further fire to your inspiration and encouraging you to pick them up and paint with thread.

## THE ESSENTIALS

### EMBROIDERY THREAD (FLOSS)

The embroidery thread (floss) I always recommend is DMC stranded embroidery cotton (floss). There are 500 colours to choose from and the sheen gives your embroidery a beautiful high-quality finish. It has six divisible strands, which allows you to vary the weight of your stitches. I always use one strand at a time as this gives me the most detailed, painterly effect. If you would like to embroider with more speed, try using two or three strands at a time.

It's always a good idea to organize your thread! You can do this any way you prefer, but personally I prefer bobbins. This way you can remember which colour is which by labelling your bobbin with the name or number, and everything stays tidier when your start embroidering your project.

### FABRIC

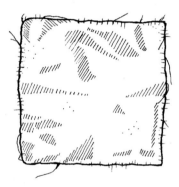

My choice of fabric is of a medium weight with a close weave (not too flimsy, but not so heavy that it is hard to pull your needle through). Please do not use a fabric that has any stretch in it – you won't achieve the required tension in the hoop, and your stitches will be very distorted.

Working with a lighter shade of fabric makes it much easier to trace the pattern. Cotton and linen fabrics are ideal to use as they are affordable and look great! I've included information about the fabric I've chosen in each project, with ideas and tips for alternative colours.

## NEEDLES

I recommend using Size 10 embroidery needles. The thinner the needle, the easier it is to embroider through the dense amounts of stitches that build up as you embroider. You will become faster at threading the needle over time, but you may just need patience at the beginning. Alternatively, you can go up to a Size 5, which has a larger eye. It's important that you feel comfortable from the start, and over time you may find your own preference.

As soon as you find your needle becomes tarnished, or you are struggling to get your needle through the fabric, it's time to change to a fresh one, so keep plenty of spares to hand. When purchasing needles, look for ones with an elongated eye for easier threading, and make sure they have a sharp point.

14

## PENCIL

When transferring a pattern to fabric (see Transferring the Patterns), my preferred tool is a traditional graphite pencil. You can sharpen a pencil to an extremely fine point, which helps with tracing the finer details of the patterns onto your fabric. If you happen to have a set of pencils, use a 2B or higher. A standard HB pencil will work, but a softer 6B will show up more on the fabric without having to press too hard.

If you make a tiny mistake, dab a little white adhesive putty onto the fabric to fade the line (the line may not disappear altogether, but should be much less noticeable).

## EMBROIDERY SCISSORS

A small pair of scissors is essential for delicate embroideries. Their small but oh-so sharp pointed blades are perfect not only for cutting lengths of thread, but also for wiggling under stitches you want to remove (although this will rarely happen!). I recommend using a good-quality pair made of stainless steel, which will snip through your thread with ease and precision, avoiding the frayed fibres that can make threading a needle very tricky.

### DID YOU KNOW?

*Embroidery scissors are stork-shaped as they were originally a staple part of a midwife's kit in the 1800s. Doing embroidery helped to pass the time waiting for labour to begin, and the scissors gradually migrated from the birthing kit to the sewing kit.*

## HOOP

The most important factor when choosing a hoop is that its job is to hold your fabric drum-tight. I like to use good-quality wooden hoops as they grip the fabric well and the screw is sturdy and strong, keeping the fabric tightly held as you stitch. It's important that the fabric doesn't loosen as you embroider as this can cause unsightly puckering in the fabric. If you are struggling to get the fabric tight in the hoop, consider wrapping self-adhesive fabric tape around the inner hoop before placing your fabric and the outer hoop over it. The tape will give the hoop extra grip.

For display purposes, I will often use a wood stain to alter the colour to suit my aesthetic. Try to choose one that says satin or waterproof on the tin. See How to Finish for more details.

15

Tools & Materials

## NICE TO HAVE

### DAYLIGHT LAMP

Purchasing a special light isn't necessary, but I can't stress enough how useful a white light source can be. It reduces eye strain and helps you to see colours accurately. If you are on a budget, purchase a cool light, halogen or daylight bulb to place in an overhead lamp. Or, invest in a daylight magnifying lamp (these are often designed with needlework in mind). I used a standard halogen bulb in a household lamp for three years before purchasing a magnifying lamp, and it worked just fine!

### NEEDLE MINDER

This is a useful magnetic tool for holding your needles in place without the fear of losing them. The front and back of the needle minder 'sandwich' your fabric while in the hoop, and also makes a very convenient placeholder. They look adorable too! Pictured is one of my own needle minders, available in my shop.

### SEAM RIPPER

For those moments when you want to remove a stitch, but the scissors aren't quite cutting it. Seam rippers are extra sharp so be careful not to accidentally cut a hole in your fabric. Personally I prefer to use scissors, but if the stitches are extra dense, a seam ripper is handy to have around!

## SOURCING YOUR KIT

I know it can be daunting purchasing your materials. You head to town for supplies, or begin your search online, and think to yourself…where do I start?!? Hopefully the following will give you a helping hand! I am based in Warwickshire, UK, and try to buy my supplies locally. If you're based elsewhere in the world, look for suppliers near you too.

### THREAD (FLOSS)

You can find embroidery thread (floss) in your local haberdashery, or online shops like eBay and Etsy. If you can't get hold of DMC, I suggest using Anchor thread as an alternative. There are online conversion charts to help you choose substitutions for the DMC shades I have used.

### NEEDLES

I personally use John James needles – they last a long time and don't tarnish easily. I also love that the company's heritage can be traced back by around 300 years, and they were founded in 1840. You don't have to purchase the same brand as me though, but I do recommend choosing a multipack with a variety of sizes if you are a beginner. The 5/10 pack of embroidery needs from John James is ideal, especially for beginners.

### FABRIC

This is probably my most asked question of all time, and to be honest, after nine years I am still searching for the perfect fabric myself. I like to visit my local haberdashery, eBay or second-hand shops when searching for natural unbleached cotton. If you're a beginner, I do recommend purchasing fabric by Kona Cotton, who have a huge variety of colours to choose from, but are on the thin side. I always add an extra layer of fabric to the back of my finished embroidery, so that you can't see the stitches on the back. It also makes the overall effect look more aesthetically pleasing.

### HOOPS

If you are based in the UK, I recommend using Elbesee or Siesta hoops as they are sturdy, long lasting and, most importantly, they hold my fabric tightly.

### MY SHOP

I occasionally sell embroidery kits in my Etsy shop, which include everything ready for you to get started: www.etsy.com/uk/shop/emillieferris.

# TRANSFERRING THE PATTERNS

All the patterns can be downloaded from:
www.davidandcharles.com

## IRON-ON PATTERNS

**1**. Select your design and remove the transfer from the back of the book, tearing carefully along the perforated strip. Trim around the transfer, leaving a small gap around the edge of about 1cm (⅜in).

**2**. Pre-press your preferred piece of fabric or item of clothing (do not use steam). Lighter-coloured fabric works best for these iron-on transfers.

**3**. Place the embroidery transfer pattern ink-side down onto the fabric. If you're worried about the design slipping as you iron, you can pin your pattern to the fabric.

**4**. Now it's time to transfer the design! Set your iron to its hottest setting (remember to turn off the steam). Carefully press the iron onto the transfer for about 40 seconds. You can take a little peak by peeling back the corner of the transfer to check that the lines have transferred correctly. Do not move the iron around as this may cause bleeding.

**5**. You are now ready to place your fabric into your embroidery hoop and begin stitching!

18

## TRACE-ON PATTERNS

**1**. Select your design and print it out. Make sure your printer's settings are set to 100% size. To double check, compare the design dimensions in the project to your freshly printed template.

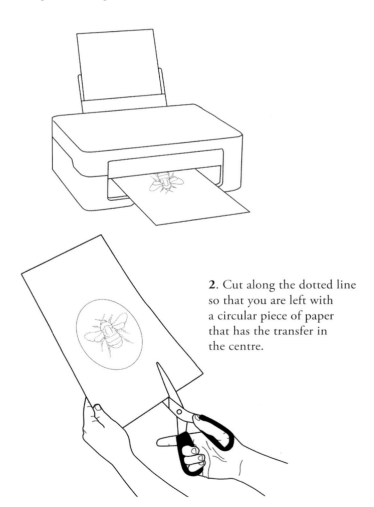

**2**. Cut along the dotted line so that you are left with a circular piece of paper that has the transfer in the centre.

<u>TIP</u>

*The transfer ink could fade over time, so it's best to iron it on just before use.*

**3.** Place down your inner hoop (the part of the hoop without the screw) down onto a flat surface. Centre the fabric over the hoop, then place the outer hoop (with the screw) on top of the first hoop and fabric. Make sure the weave of your fabric is running vertically and horizontally in the hoop. Keep pulling the fabric on opposite sides while slowly tightening the screw each time. The screw should be wound as tightly as possible, with the fabric being drum-tight to the touch.

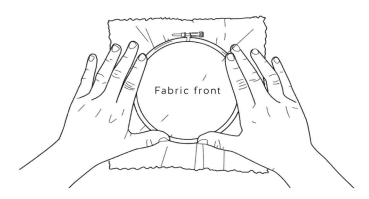

Fabric front

**5.** With the paper template attached to the back of the fabric, you are ready to trace the pattern. When held up to a source of light you should be able to see the outline. You can hold up the hoop to a lamp or window. After you begin tracing, it's important that you do not move the piece of paper, even once. Trace the pattern with a sharp pencil until it is complete, then remove the piece of paper. Be careful to not leave any adhesive putty behind on the fabric.

You are now ready to embroider!

19

**4.** Take the circular paper template you cut out in Step 1, locate the four lines printed on the outer corners, and lightly secure four tiny blobs of white adhesive putty to the front. Flip your hoop so that you are looking at the back and lightly place the piece of paper front-side down onto the back of the

Fabric back

fabric. When held up to the light and viewed from the front of the hoop, you should be able to check that the pattern is centred in the hoop. Keep adjusting until you are happy.

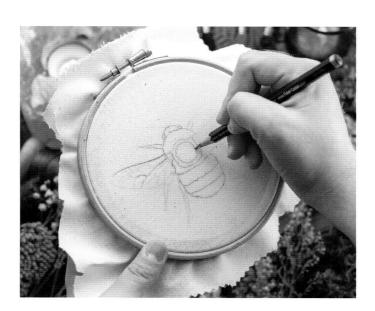

Transferring the Patterns

# STITCH GUIDE

You need very few embroidery techniques to achieve the finish you can see in this book. The most important is Long-and-Short Stitch, but the others provide the definition, texture and decoration that help the painterly effect to pop from the fabric!

## PAINTING WITH LONG-AND-SHORT STITCH

This is an embroidery technique that is fantastic for filling large surface areas of fabric. Long-and-Short Stitch is essentially like painting, but rather than using paint on paper, you are using thread on fabric. The clever shading effect is achieved using a different embroidery thread (floss) colour in each row, creating a painterly effect much like brushstrokes.

So how do you paint with Long-and-Short Stitch? You are essentially embroidering one short stitch, then one long stitch, then another short stitch, another long stitch and so on, alternating the two lengths to build a series of staggered rows in different colours. There is no need to worry about making all the long stitches equal length, or the short stitch equal. The more you stagger your stitches using different lengths, the better it looks. You want the longer stitches to be squeezing their way into each other's rows. The stitches should be tightly packed together, but not overlapping (although it's not the end of the world if they are!). You don't want to see any spaces between the stitches.

**Long-and-Short Stitch**

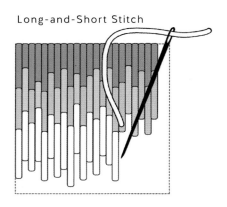

Stitch Guide

1. Begin by locating the best place to start your first row – this is usually along the outline of the pattern. In this example, I'm starting along the inner edge of this marked square (**fig. 1**).

2. To create a crisp line, use Split Back Stitch (see Stitch Guide: Split Back Stitch) to outline the edge of the shape perpendicular to the planned Long-and-Short Stitch (**Fig. 2**). The instructions will tell you which colour to use.

3. Select your first thread (floss) colour according to the instructions and Colour Guide, and thread your needle with a knot on the end (see Starting to Stitch). Starting just outside the line of Split Back Stitch, come up from the back of the fabric to the front to make your first stitch (this can be a long or short stitch – it's up to you!). Then stitch another line, adjacent to the first but with a different stitch length. Continue alternating Long-and-Short Stitches until you have a row of stitches with no gaps (**fig. 3**).

4. The instructions and Colour Guide will tell you whether your next row should be the same colour, or a different one. In this case I want to build up more of the black. So, work some stitches from the edge to fill any gaps in the first row as we did in Step 3, and again alternating Long-and-Short Stitches, completely cover the fabric as the colour begins to "brush" across the fabric (**fig. 4**).

5. Switching to grey allows you to see in detail how the rows of Long-and-Short Stitch dovetail with each other. The effect is very organic but precise as we build the grey stitches. Now that the outline is completely covered, we use only the previous row as a guide, ensuring that every gap in the previous row of black stitching is filled (**fig. 5**).

6. Again, I work two or three rows of grey until I have covered the space indicated on the Colour Guide (**fig. 6**).

7. The final colour in this block of stitching will be white, so outline along the edge using Split Back Stitch in white thread (floss) in exactly the same way as we did with black in Step 2. After one or two rows of white Long-and-Short Stitch, do the opposite of Step 3, taking the last row of stitches just over the Split Back Stitch before pushing the needle down through the fabric. Once the whole edge is covered, as is the stitched area itself, you can finish stitching (see How to Finish) (**fig. 7**).

| fig. 1 | fig. 2 | fig. 3 |
|---|---|---|
| fig. 4 | fig. 5 | fig. 6 |

fig. 7

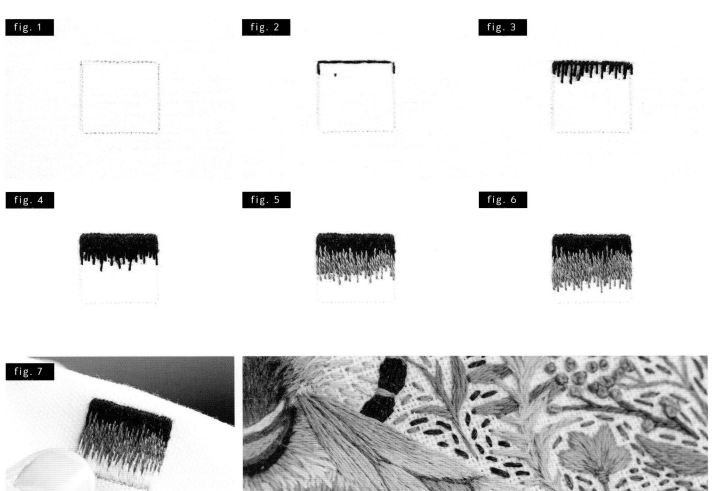

### TIP

*Refer to the Photo Guide of the finished stitching for further guidance, but your stitching will look different to mine, and that of every other stitcher – this is freestyle embroidery, remember!*

Stitch Guide

## EMBROIDERING AROUND CURVES

Shading doesn't always follow straight lines, but you still have to follow these lines in the most natural way possible.

For example, if there is a curve, you can begin to angle your rows in a different direction - the same way that water flows around a river bend. By following the curve around with the thread, it will create a more natural look. This is especially important when embroidering animals, people and plants. Make sure you embroider in the direction of natural curves, the growth pattern of fur and so on. Each design has a Stitch Direction diagram to help you achieve the desired effect. This is key to taking your results to the next level. If you get caught up making your embroidery neat and straight without changing the direction, it can look very unnatural.

24

## STRAIGHT STITCH

Take any single stitch from a block of Long-and-Short Stitch, and you have a Straight Stitch.

I've used Straight Stitch several times throughout the projects, not only to add detail and emphasize certain features, but also as a purely decorative stitch. Use this stitch like a single brush-stroke of paint wherever indicated by the project instructions and template. However, if you want to experiment with different lengths and add your own painterly touches here and there, feel free!

25

## SPLIT BACK STITCH

Simple to learn, Split Back Stitch is not a filling stitch, but is instead used for outlines.

It is quite simple to get the hang of, and great for outlines. Pull your thread up from the back of the fabric (a) and make a stitch in the opposite direction to which the line will follow (b). Come back up in the opposite direction in front of the first stitch (c), and go back down through the middle of the first stitch (d). Continue doing this until the line is complete. The trick to making this stitch look good is to make the stitches as tiny as you can when following curved lines.

## FRENCH KNOTS

French Knots are useful for creating seeds, textures and even adding interest to background spaces. I use two or three strands of thread for French Knots.

After anchoring or knotting your thread, pull your thread to the front of the fabric (a). With your free hand, hold the thread tautly upwards near the base of the fabric. With your other hand, push the needle against the taut thread and wind the thread round two or three times (b).

Whilst still holding the thread up and taut with your free hand, begin to push the needle into the fabric (c). Aim the needle as close as possible to where you originally came upwards and pull it through (d). Voilà! You should have a French Knot!

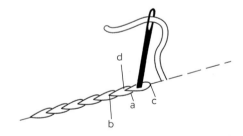

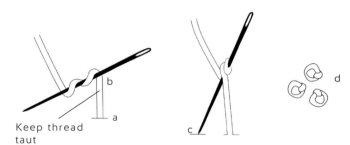

Keep thread
taut

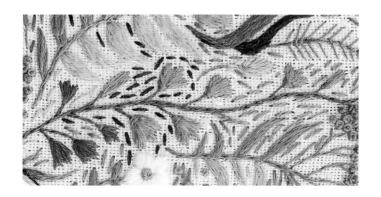

# SATIN STITCH

When a smoother colour-block effect is required than Long-and-Short Stitch can achieve, Satin Stitch is ideal.

Outline the object with Split Back Stitch (in the same way you used it before starting Long-and-Short Stitch) to make the finished embroidery neater (**a**). Then using one or two strands of cotton (floss), start at one end of the object by anchoring your thread inside the lines. Come up through the fabric just outside the Split Back Stitch (**b**) and across the whole object horizontally until you reach the other side of the stitch – push your needle down here (**c**). Keep repeating this step, ensuring you start each stitch on the same side, which in this case means coming back up at (**d**), then down again at (**e**). Don't come back up on the same side your needle went in. Keep your stitches close together so that you have no gaps, and finish filling in the object.

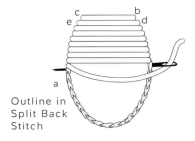

Outline in
Split Back
Stitch

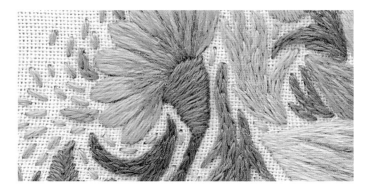

Stitch Guide

# STARTING TO STITCH

Before you begin stitching, there are a few simple techniques that will make your embroidery easier, neater and more beautiful. That way you'll enjoy the process as well as the results!

## PREPARING THE THREAD (FLOSS)

The embroidery thread (floss) comes as six divisible strands (see Tools & Materials), so you will need to cut it to length and sort out the strands.

**1**. First, slowly pull the length of thread you're going to use from the skein, still in its six-strand form **(fig. 1)**. I recommend cutting it to the same length as your forearm – this ensures you can pull the thread all the way through the fabric to form each stitch, which helps to avoid tangles and keeps your stitches neat.

**2**. Now separate one strand of thread from the six. Do this by holding the skein lightly but firmly in one hand, and use the other hand to separate a single strand from the skein and gently pull it through your fingers until it comes free **(fig. 2)**. Now you are ready to thread the needle!

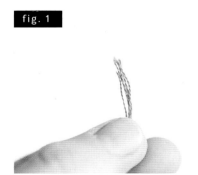

fig. 1

fig. 2

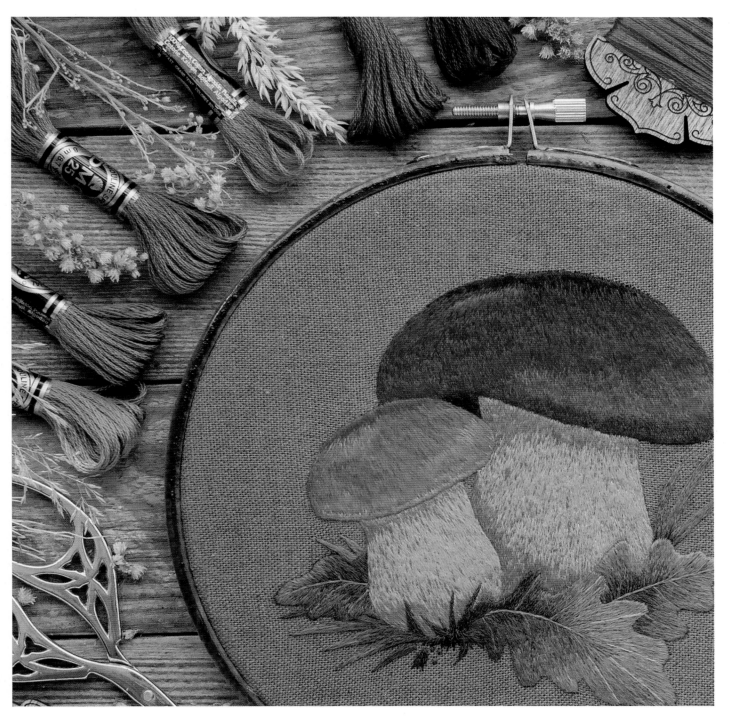

29

Starting to Stitch

## THREADING THE NEEDLE

Threading the needle can sometimes be the most frustrating part for beginners, but please do not fret. The method I use is simple:

**1.** To create as fine a point as possible at the end of the thread, dampen the tip on a wet kitchen towel or in a small cup of water.

**2.** Hold the thread between your thumb and index finger, and pinch it firmly until you can barely see the end **(fig. 3)**.

**3.** Your fingers are now supporting the thread, giving you a rigid point that is easier to control. You should now be able to ease the thread through the eye of the needle **(fig. 4)**. Pull the thread through the needle by about 5cm (2in).

## BEGINNING AND ENDING A STITCH (HOW TO ANCHOR YOUR THREAD)

These are my preferred options for securing the thread before you start stitching, and when you come to the end of the thread on your needle.

**OPTION A: MAKING A KNOT**

This is the simplest and quickest method to start and end your stitches. However, this method means your embroidery may not withstand the length of time, due to knots unravelling.

**1.** After threading your needle leaving a 5cm (2in) tail, add a tiny knot or two at the other end, furthest from the needle **(fig. 5)**.

**2.** Begin embroidering your desired stitch, following the instructions in the project and the Stitch Guide when needed.

**3.** When you have nearly used up the whole length of thread on your needle, make sure there is enough left to create a knot. Take your thread to the back of the hoop and begin to tie a knot. I put my needle into the loop of the knot to slide it down as close to the fabric as possible before gently but firmly pulling the knot tight **(fig. 6)**. Then, using your scissors, trim the tail as close to the knot as possible, otherwise the tail may get tangled up in stitches later.

30

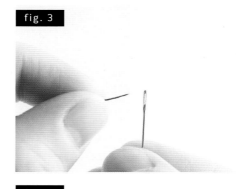

fig. 3

fig. 4

fig. 5

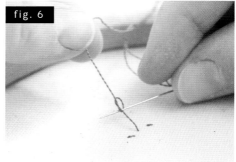

fig. 6

## OPTION B: WITHOUT A KNOT

If your embroidery is going to hang untouched on your wall or displayed on a shelf, then a knot will suffice. However, if you are embroidering directly on to clothes, or are making a patch, then it's worth getting into the habit of using this anchoring method instead.

**1.** Choose a location close to where you want to start embroidering. It's important that this is within the pattern outlines, as you it needs to be covered with embroidery.

**2.** Without making a knot at the end of the thread, make the tiniest stitch you can on the fabric (**fig. 7**) – this is the first stage of your anchoring stitch. You should now have the tiniest little tail of thread on the back of our fabric (**fig. 8**).

**3.** Come back up through the fabric close to the first stitch (**fig. 9**) then back down through the centre of that same stitch (**fig. 10**). You will be left with a tiny anchored stitch (**fig. 11**). You can see how this is used to anchor thread in the Sunflower design (**fig. 12**). Now just cut off the tiny tail on the back and embroider to your heart's content!

**4.** You can finish the same way, creating an anchor stitch hidden in the existing embroidery. I still use knots much of the time, though, as old habits die hard! So, if you have any problems with this method, please feel free to make a knot instead.

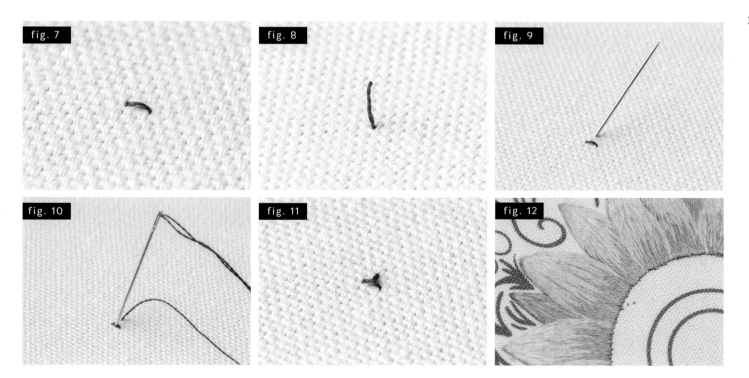

fig. 7

fig. 8

fig. 9

fig. 10

fig. 11

fig. 12

Starting to Stitch

# Time to Stitch...

With the basics under your belt, all you have to do now is choose your template from the end of the book, gather your thread, tighten your hoop and begin!

DANDELION

SUNFLOWER

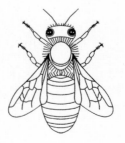

## TIP

*There are templates for the Honey Bee, Sunflower and Robin both with and without backgrounds for even more creative possibilities!*

MUSHROOM

ROBIN

HONEY BEE

Time to Stitch...

# THE PROJECTS

*"The year is a book, isn't it, Marilla? Spring's pages are written in Mayflowers and violets, summer's in roses, autumn's in red maple leaves, and winter in holly and evergreens."* —
**L.M. Montgomery, *Anne of Green Gables* (1908)**

Nature and the ever-changing seasons are an abundant source of inspiration for me, so what better way to celebrate them than here. There are five projects in total, four of them symbolizing spring, summer, autumn and winter. And as our final project, we have a special guest – the spellbinding Honey Bee. Of the insect realm, this creature is my favourite – it brings me so much joy to embroider, encapsulating beautifully the essence of nature.

When I designed each piece, I took inspiration from its season while also creating artwork to suit your home or clothing year round. The flora can easily be changed to suit your own aesthetic, and I highly encourage you to do so. Choosing the colours for a project is one of the great joys in creating artwork that feels distinctively you.

Take your time and enjoy the process.

Happy stitching, friends!

# DANDELION

*"What I need is the dandelion in the spring. The bright yellow that means rebirth instead of destruction. The promise that life can go on, no matter how bad our losses. That it can be good again."* — **Suzanne Collins,** *Mockingjay* **(2010)**

This pattern honours the cheerful dandelion. They turn our lawns into fields of gold, providing tasty nectar for the butterflies, hoverflies, bees and other insects alike. Seeing them brings a smile to my face – they indicate that spring has arrived and I can enjoy sunnier, warmer countryside walks. Dandelions remind me that joy can be found in the simple, everyday moments of life. They symbolize perseverance, healing, freedom, humility and innocence.

As dandelions turn to seed, I feel nostalgic for childhood days when I would close my eyes and make a wish, feeling pure delight at seeing the seeds blow into the air. In this beginner-friendly design there is lots of room for novice mistakes, and the end result is beautiful even if your stitches aren't neat. Focus on getting used to transitioning between the different-but-similar colours; this is also one of my favourite parts of embroidery – creating subtle colour blends!

If you wish, the pattern can be simplified by using fewer shades for the leaves. I recommend using only the DMC shades 937 and 3345. You won't have to buy as much thread, and fewer colour changes allow a faster finish. I think this design looks great on a dark background. The cotton I used is available in a wide range of colours, and is thin enough to trace the pattern. On this colour, I used a white artist's pen, but you could use a white pencil or gel pen. If your fabric is too thick to see through, you can transfer the design onto fabric using a water-soluble stabilizer, a type of transfer paper you print directly onto before attaching to your fabric. Happy stitching!

## YOU WILL NEED

### EMBROIDERY COTTON (FLOSS)

A total of 14 skeins of DMC stranded cotton in the following colours. You'll require only one skein of each colour.

- **Greens** 612 - 319 - 3347 - 3364 - 3345 - 937 - 469
- **Teals** 520 - 501
- **Yellows** 783 - 3820
- **Oranges** 3826 - 782
- **Light grey** 648

### FABRIC

One square no smaller than 30 x 30cm (12 x 12in). I used Robert Kaufman's 100% Kona Cotton in the shade Indigo.

### HOOP

15cm (6in) diameter

### NEEDLE

Size 5–10 embroidery needle (I used Size 10)

### STITCHES USED:

- Long-and-Short Stitch
- Straight Stitch
- French Knot
- Split Back Stitch

See also the Stitch Direction Guide

### STITCHING TIME

Approx. 12–15 hours

### SIZE OF FINISHED EMBROIDERY

Approx. 14.8cm (5⅞in) diameter, displayed in a 15cm (6in) hoop.

## BEFORE YOU BEGIN...

- Transfer the design template onto your fabric as described in Transferring the Patterns, or use the iron-on transfer paper included with the book. With the design placed centrally, mount the fabric in the hoop and tighten the screw as shown.

- If using the colour palette provided (rather than your own), refer to the Colour Guide as you stitch.

- Check the Stitch Direction guide to ensure your stitches are lying correctly.

- Unless specified otherwise, use one strand of cotton (floss) taken from the six divisible strands. See Starting to Stitch for more information.

## STITCH DIRECTION

# COLOUR GUIDE

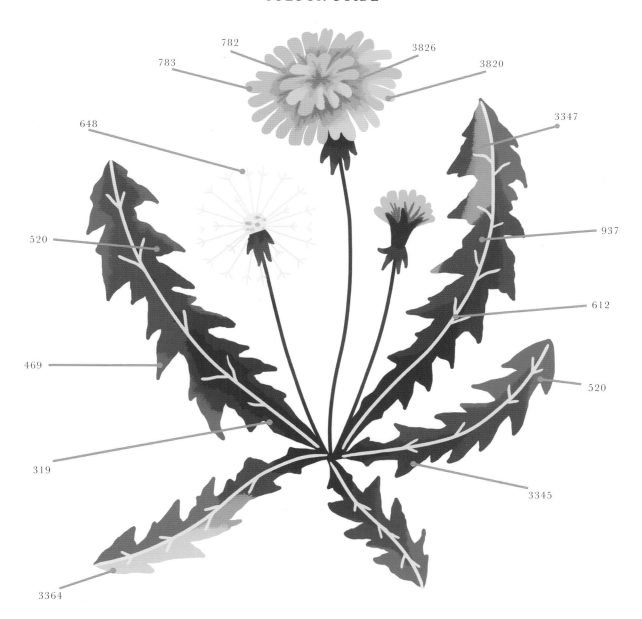

782
783
3826
3820
648
3347
520
937
469
612
319
520
3364
3345

39

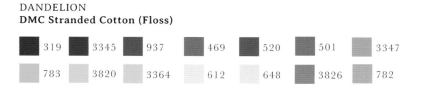

DANDELION
**DMC Stranded Cotton (Floss)**

| | | | | | | |
|---|---|---|---|---|---|---|
| 319 | 3345 | 937 | 469 | 520 | 501 | 3347 |
| 783 | 3820 | 3364 | 612 | 648 | 3826 | 782 |

Dandelion

40

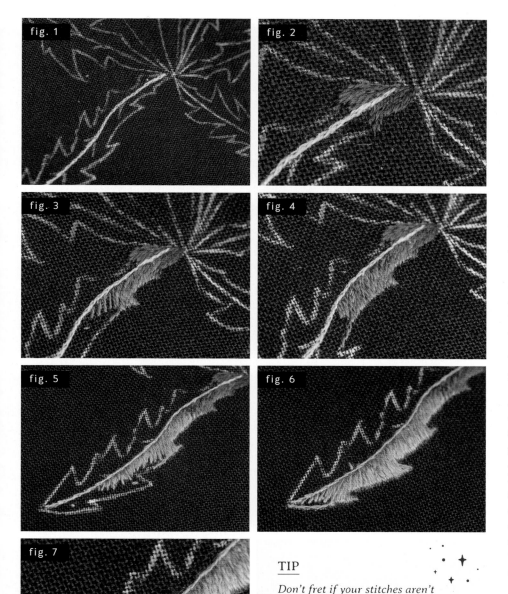

fig. 1

fig. 2

fig. 3

fig. 4

fig. 5

fig. 6

fig. 7

## STITCHING THE LEAVES AND STEMS

**1.** Begin with the leaf positioned at seven o'clock. Thread your needle with one strand of green **612** and prepare to stitch (see Starting to Stitch). Use Split Back Stitch to embroider the main central vein (**fig. 1**). Don't worry about making it super neat, as you will be going over it again later once you have embroidered the leaves themselves.

**2.** Fill in the left-hand side of the leaf first. To start, thread your needle with one strand of green **319** and use Long-and-Short Stitch to begin filling the leaf as pictured (**fig. 2**). Try to follow the same stitch direction that I am using to create a more realistic looking leaf (see Stitch Direction Guide for more help). Then switch to teal **520** (**fig. 3**), followed by **501** (**fig. 4**).

**3.** To complete this half of the leaf, carry on in the same way using Long-and-Short Stitch. First, transition to green **3347** as shown (**fig. 5**) then to **3364**. Again, outline the tip of the leaf using Split Back Stitch in the same colour (**fig. 6**). Ensure the tip of the leaf is brought to a point for definition, with your Long-and-Short Stitch directed from the centre of the leaf to just beyond the Split Back Stitch (**fig. 7**).

### TIP

*Don't fret if your stitches aren't indentical to mine. Even if I embroidered this design a second time, it wouldn't be an exact copy. Be kind to yourself as you stitch, just as you would be patient with a child.*

Dandelion

4. Now we'll fill in the left-hand side of the leaf, starting with green **319** (**fig. 8**). As you move up the leaf, transition to teal **520** (**fig. 9**), then on to **501** (**fig. 10**).

5. To add extra dimension to the leaf, you can add an additional shade of green as I did. I stitched a few flecks of green **3345** to the right-hand side to break up the teal shade **501**. Then, on the left-hand side, I used the same green and technique to add more depth along the centre of the leaf. To finish, go over the vein again, using Split Back Stitch in green **612**. Refer back to the original pattern to position the small offshoots, again using Split Back Stitch (**fig. 11**).

6. Moving in a clockwise direction, you can now begin the next leaf. As before, fill in the centre vein using Split Back Stitch in green **612**. Begin to fill in the leaf using Long-and-Short Stitch, starting with green **319** then moving on to **3345** as shown (**fig. 12**). Complete this second colour (**fig. 13**)

TIP

*Feel free to get creative with the veins, experiment by adding more as I did, or use different shades of green.*

42

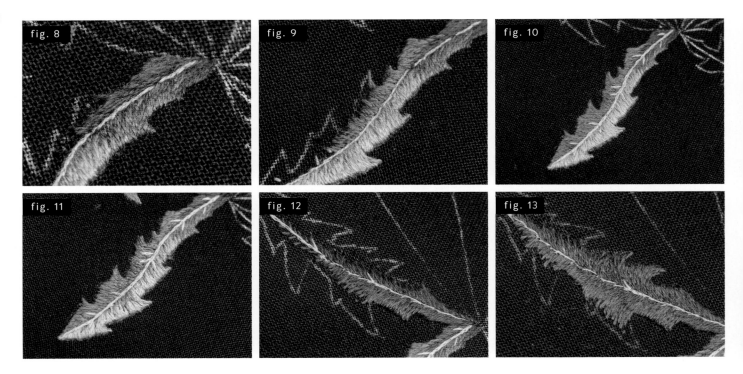

The Projects

7. If you're finding it difficult to keep your stitches tidy as you reach the outer edges of the leaf, you can outline the leaf using Split Back Stitch first (**fig. 14**). Then when filling the area using Long-and-Short Stitch, take your needle just beyond the outline. Continue to fill the area as pictured, transitioning from green **937** to **469** (**fig. 15**).

8. Begin to fill in the teal shades starting with **501** on the edge of the leaf (**fig. 16**). Then continue to fill in using **520** (**fig. 17**). If you don't place your colours in exactly the same way I did, it doesn't matter too much. The blending effect on the finished piece will still be the same.

9. Fill in the left-hand side of the leaf with Long-and-Short Stitch using green **937**. Then use Split Back Stitch in the same colour to define the outline as before (**fig. 18**). Complete this side of the leaf using green **469**, covering the outline as you stitch (**fig. 19**).

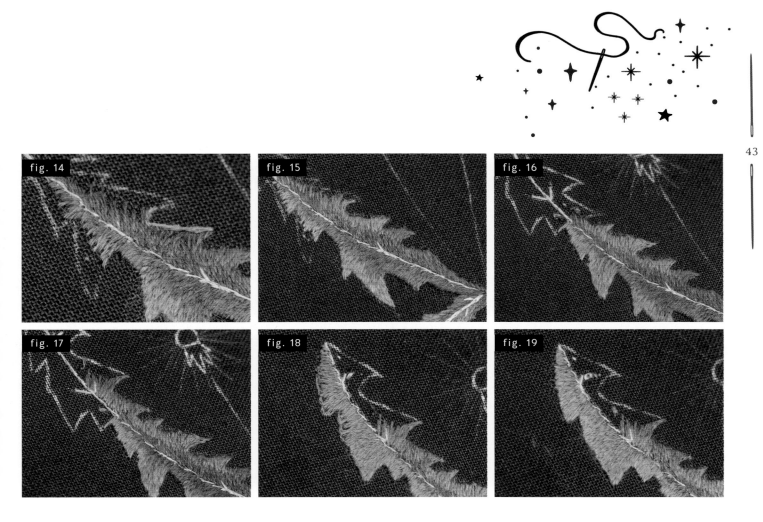

fig. 14  fig. 15  fig. 16

fig. 17  fig. 18  fig. 19

Dandelion

**10.** Finish the right-hand side of the leaf with Long-and-Short Stitch using green **520**. Again, use Split Back Stitch in the same colour to define the outline **(fig. 20)**. Use Long-and-Short Stitch in teal **501** to fill in the rest, again hiding the Split Back Stitch outline. Use the same colour to add flecks of this cooler colour to the edges of the leaf **(fig. 21)**. Finish the leaf in same way as before, using Split Back Stitch in green **612** to re-define the centre vein.

**11.** I imagine by now you have gotten quite into the swing of things embroidering the leaves. However, I will continue to guide you through, making the stitching process as relaxing as possible.

Move on to the five o'clock leaf and fill it from the base to the tip with Long-and-Short Stitch in following order: green **319**, **3345**, **937** and **469.** To keep your stitches along the outer edges neat, don't forget to outline the shape in the same colour you'll use to fill it in **(fig. 22)**. Add the finishing touch by defining the vein as before, using Split Back Stitch in green **612** (although I'm sure I don't need to tell you that anymore!) **(fig. 23)**.

fig. 20

fig. 21

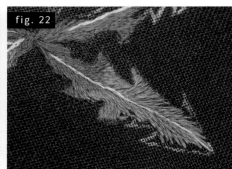
fig. 22

fig. 23

### TIP

*For a realistic colour palette, contrast hot and cold to give the viewer a sense of depth, avoiding a flat effect. This is seen in the warmer yellow-green and colder blue-green shades in the leaves.*

The Projects

**12.** Now fill in the three o'clock leaf, starting on the right-hand side with Long-and-Short Stitch. First, graduate from green **319** to **3345**, then repeat on the left-hand side **(fig. 24)**. On the right-hand side, continue stitching, graduating from teal **520** to **501**. On the left-hand side, continue stitching, graduating from green **937** to **469 (fig. 25)**. Use the outlining technique to keep the edges neat all the way to the tip, and add a few scatters of teal **501** on the right, and green **469** on the left **(fig. 26)**. You've nearly finished the leaves! One more to go…

**13.** As I was embroidering with green **319** and **3345** of the leaf in the previous step, I used the already-threaded needle to stitch the stems at the same time. You can embroider these at any stage, but I did them at this stage to save thread. When you're ready, fill in the dandelion stems in Split Back Stitch, using two strands of thread (the stems wouldn't look realistic or strong enough to hold up the weight of the dandelion head using one only strand).

To embroider the stems, I started with green **319** at the base of each stem, changing to **3345**, then back to **319** to mimic the shadow cast by the dandelion head **(fig. 27)**. To add dimension, I embroidered Split Back Stitch along the right-hand side of each stem using just one strand of the lighter shade of green **937 (fig. 28)**.

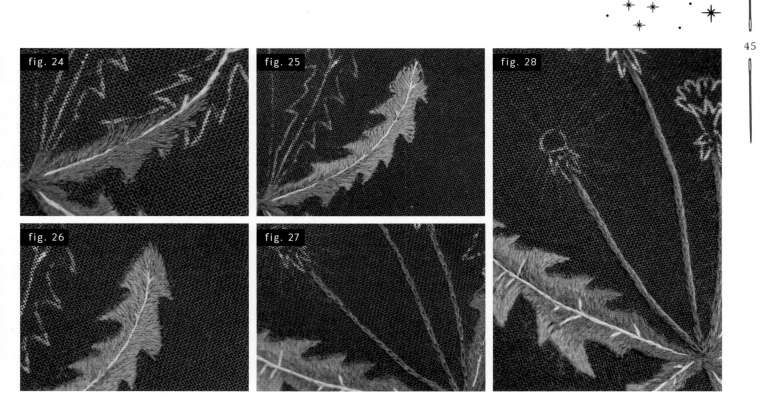

fig. 24

fig. 25

fig. 28

fig. 26

fig. 27

Dandelion

**14.** Fill in the remaining leaf with Long-and-Short Stitch, beginning by graduating the colours on the right-hand side from green **319** to **3345**, **937** and **469**. Graduate on the left-hand side from green **319** to **3345**, **937** and **3347** (**fig. 29**) (**fig. 30**). Finish with green **937** on the outer edge, then complete the leaf with Split Back Stitch down the centre using green **612** (**fig. 31**).

**15.** After completing all the leaves, I wanted to add extra detailing and contrast to them. To achieve this, I went back over every leaf using Split Back Stitch in the shade green **319** to add extra contour along the centre of each one (**fig. 32**). This extra touch is optional of course – if you're happy with the way your leaves look, then skip ahead to the next step!

**16.** Before completing the flower heads, add a line of Split Back Stitch in green **937** along their stalks to create dimension (**fig. 33**).

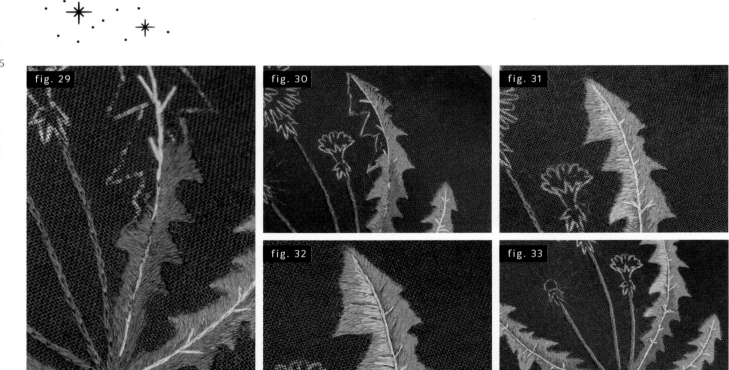

fig. 29

fig. 30

fig. 31

fig. 32

fig. 33

The Projects

## STITCHING THE FLOWER HEADS

**17.** Fill in the green parts of the flower heads using vertical Long-and-Short Stitch – refer to the Stitch Guide for more detail on the directions of the stitches. I used green **319** and **3345 (fig. 34)**, then **937 (fig. 35)** to create lifelike light and shadow.

**18.** Fill in the right-hand dandelion head using Long-and-Short Stitch. Begin with orange **3826** at the base, followed by **783 (fig. 36)**. Try to follow the same stitch direction as I did for the best results.

**19.** It's time to stitch the main dandelion head! You want to create the illusion of sunlight hitting the outermost petals, so begin by adding the lightest yellow **3820** to the tips of the petals **(fig. 37)**. Once this lightest yellow is complete, continue using the same stitch to add the slightly darker **783 (fig. 38)**.

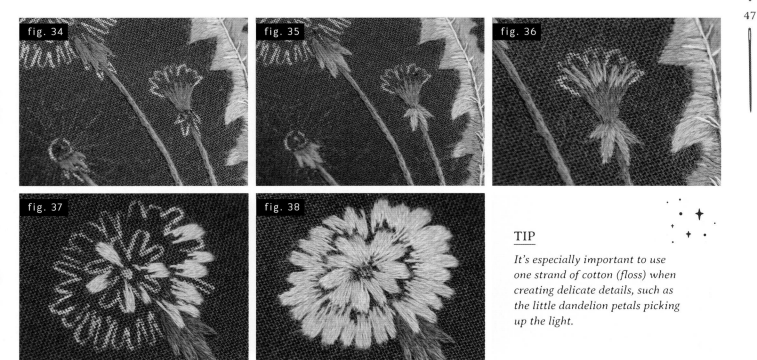

fig. 34 fig. 35 fig. 36 fig. 37 fig. 38

### TIP

*It's especially important to use one strand of cotton (floss) when creating delicate details, such as the little dandelion petals picking up the light.*

Dandelion

**20**. Keep building the depth of colour towards the bases of each petal. Carry on with Long-and-Short Stitch to add orange **782** (**fig. 39**), then transition to the warmer orange **3826** (**fig. 40**). This colour is almost orange, which adds depth and shadow to the head of the dandelion.

**21**. Now let's finish our hoop with the delicate dandelion seed head. Using the light grey **648**, use straight stitches of different lengths to form the structure (**fig. 41**).

**22**. Using the same shade, add the dandelion seeds as tiny Straight Stitches. Don't worry about your stitches looking exactly the same as mine – there's lots of room here for you to make the dandelion head as fluffy or as minimalist as you like. I added seeds to the ends of the long Straight Stitches, some part-way along, and a couple starting to float free (**fig. 42**).

**23**. Complete the centre of the dandelion seed head with a cluster of French Knots using grey **937** and green **648** (**fig. 43**).

You did it! Congratulations my stitching friend! I hope you enjoyed embroidering your dandelion and gained confidence in your abilities to paint with thread. I'm sure you did an amazing job. Take a photo and share your finished piece on social media with pride.

fig. 39

fig. 40

fig. 41

fig. 42

fig. 43

The Projects

Dandelion

# SUNFLOWER

## OUR INSPIRATION TO THRIVE

*"Rest is not idleness, and to lie sometimes on the grass on a summer day listening to the murmur of water, or watching the clouds float across the sky, is hardly a waste of time."* — **John Lubbock**

This embroidery design is in honour of the yellow, happy sunflower. I love that I now have this summer flora hanging in my home throughout the year to remind me of sunny days in the past, present and future. Sunflowers bloom during the warm summer months and brighten the mood of whomever sees them. They are a reminder to follow the light, and to let yourself grow to extraordinary heights.

This pattern is such fun and very easy to get lost in. Mistakes are easily hidden, so don't worry about getting too caught up in striving for perfection. The flurry of French Knots in the centre of the flower is so meditative and satisfying to stitch! I love how the texture of the knots clustered together emulates real sunflowers seeds. The flora in the background can also be easily adapted by using your own colour palette. I think this design would look lovely with pink flowers as an alternative, or you could create a moodier piece by using a darker shade for the background, I would recommend a dark brown, green or black. You could also easily just embroider the sunflower in the centre of a smaller hoop to shorten your stitching time. I think that would make the sweetest gift for a sunflower lover in your life. Enjoy and experiment with this one!

# YOU WILL NEED

### EMBROIDERY COTTON (FLOSS)

A total of 11 skeins of DMC stranded cotton in the following colours. You'll require only one skein of each colour.

- **Yellows** 782 - 3852 - 3820
- **Browns** 801 - 433 - 434
- **Greens** 936 - 469 - 732 - 371 - 833

### FABRIC

One square no smaller than 30 x 30cm (12 x 12in). I used Robert Kaufman's 100% Kona Cotton in the shade Snow.

### HOOP

15cm (6in) diameter

### NEEDLE

Size 5–10 embroidery needle (I used Size 10)

### STITCHES USED:

- Long-and-Short Stitch
- French Knot
- Straight Stitch
- Split Back Stitch
- Satin Stitch

See also the Stitch Direction Guide

### STITCHING TIME

Approx. 15–18 hours

### SIZE OF FINISHED EMBROIDERY

Approx. 14.8cm (5⅞in) diameter, displayed in a 15cm (6in) hoop.

# BEFORE YOU BEGIN...

- Transfer the design template onto your fabric as described in Transferring the Patterns, or use the iron-on transfer paper included with the book. With the design placed centrally, mount the fabric in the hoop and tighten the screw as shown.

- If using the colour palette provided (rather than your own), refer to the Colour Guide as you stitch.

- Check the Stitch Direction guide to ensure your stitches are lying correctly.

- Unless specified otherwise, use one strand of cotton (floss) taken from the six divisible strands. See Starting to Stitch for more information.

STITCH DIRECTION

**SUNFLOWER**
**DMC Stranded Cotton (Floss)**

| | | | | | |
|---|---|---|---|---|---|
| 936 | 469 | 732 | 371 | 833 | 801 |
| 433 | 434 | 782 | 3852 | 3820 | |

Sunflower

54

## STITCHING THE SUNFLOWER PETALS

**1**. Begin with the sunflower petals. (It doesn't matter which one you start with, as each one follows a near identical process.) Thread your needle with one strand of yellow **782** and prepare to stitch (see Starting to Stitch). Use Long-and-Short Stitch, referring to the Colour Guide to help you with colour placement if you're unsure **(Fig. 1)**.

**2**. Still using one strand and Long-and-Short Stitch, transition from yellow **782** to **3852 (Fig. 2)**. Finish the tip of the petal using yellow **3820 (Fig. 3)**

**3**. Use the darker yellow **782** to add a few extra Straight Stitches to elongate the darker shade at the base of the petal further towards the tip **(Fig. 4)**. This added light and shade creates more realistic depth, giving the petals a dimensional appearance.

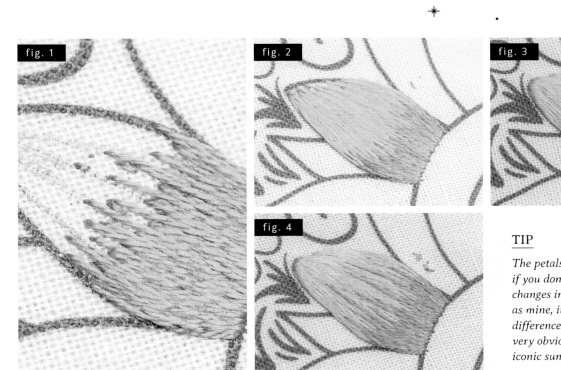

fig. 1

fig. 2

fig. 3

fig. 4

### TIP

*The petals are very forgiving, so if you don't make your colour changes in exactly the same places as mine, it won't make too much difference. The end result will still very obviously resemble a sunny, iconic sunflower.*

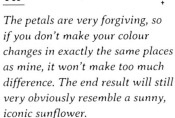

Sunflower

4. Repeat the process in Step 3 for all the other petals (**fig. 5**). There are three layers of petals with varying amounts of each petal showing. If you are unsure of how to tackle them, begin with the petals at the front of the flower head, marked (a). Then move on to the partially visible petals marked (b), and finally the petals just peeping out from the back, marked (c).

Once you have finished filling in all your petals, you might find that they merge into each other. To add back in the separation and definition needed, outline the petals using Split Back Stitch in yellow **3852**.

When stitching the petals marked (c), use the darkest yellow **782** closer to the tip as shown in the Colour Guide (**fig. 6**). In a couple of these petals, I haven't used the lightest shade of yellow **3820** at all, adding further realistic shadow and dimension to the embroidery.

## STITCHING THE SUNFLOWER CENTRE

5. The first step is to outline the centre of the sunflower using French Knots in the darkest brown **801** (**fig. 7**). I used two strands of thread, wrapping them around the needle twice (see the Stitch Guide). Experiment and use more than two strands if you wish.

For the initial outline, I placed my French Knots just inside the outline formed by the base of the petals, rather than directly onto it (**fig. 8**). The French Knots should fill the inner space, but not cover where the stitched petals are. However, if you do find your French Knots creeping over a little into the petal area, you can leave them.

fig. 5

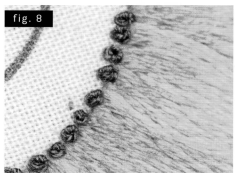

fig. 8

fig. 6

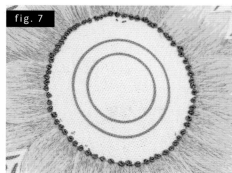

fig. 7

## TIP

*Due to the random nature of the French Knots, this process should be relaxing – please don't worry about things being perfect! Some knots can be larger, some smaller! Our biggest goal is to fill every gap.*

56

**6**. Now you've finished outlining the centre, begin to fill in this area using the slightly lighter shade of brown **433 (fig. 9)**. Continue working in circles until you have filled the area indicated on the pattern with brown **433 (fig. 10)**.

As you fill in with the French Knots, you will start to get a sense of a how much space each individual knot fills. The knots should be touching each other just enough to cover the gaps.

**7**. Fill in the narrower, second circle using the next lightest brown **434 (fig. 11)**. Then go back to the darkest shade of brown **801** and fill the centre of the sunflower with French Knots **(fig. 12)**. Once you have filled the centre of the sunflower French Knots, it's worth giving it a final check for gaps. If the gap is very small you can create a tiny French Knot by using two strands of thread as before, but this time wrapping them around your needle only once.

**8**. To add extra contrast to the petals and draw the eye to them from the more deeply shaded centre, use brown **434** to add vertical lines of Straight Stitch as I have **(fig. 13)**. Follow the curve of each petal, keeping the longest line to the centre of each one to emphasize the shape.

Sunflower

## STITCHING THE DECORATIVE FLOWER HEADS

**9.** Begin to fill in the smaller decorative flowers with yellow **782**, using Long-and-Short Stitch and working up from the base of the flower **(fig. 14)**. Follow with the slightly lighter yellow **3852** to fill the petals to the tip **(fig. 15)**. If you'd like to add extra definition, use brown **434** to add Straight Stitches or Split Back Stitches, to separate and define the individual petals **(fig. 16)**. Repeat this process to fill in all six decorative flower heads.

## STITCHING THE SUNFLOWER LEAVES

**10.** Move down to the base of the main sunflower, and fill in the stem with green **936**, using Long-and-Short Stitch and two strands. Then using the same shade and Long-and-Short Stitch again, outline the lower edge of the leaf using two strands of thread. Fill the lower half of the leaf, using two stands of green **936** **(fig. 17)**. I used Satin Stitch for these leaves, which creates a smoother looking surface than Long-and-Short Stitch would. Refer to the Stitch

Direction guide to ensure your stitches are angled correctly all down the length of the leaf to ensure a dimensional effect that mimics the contours of real leaves. Repeat for the other leaf **(fig. 18)**.

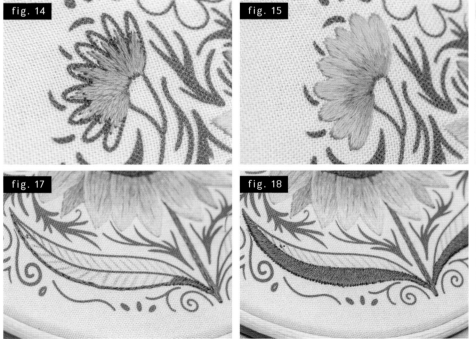

## TIP

*If you know any other line stitches such as Stem Stitch or Chain Stitch, these are also great for filling in flower stems or curved lines. Personally, I'm just as happy using Split Back Stitch.*

**11.** Fill in the upper half of both leaves with green **469.** Use the same technique as before, outlining them in Split Back Stitch and filling them in using continuous Long-and-Short Stitch (**fig. 19**). Use Split Back Stitch in green **371** to add the veins; use just one strand of thread to create this finer detail (**fig. 20**).

**12.** Once I had created the main body of these sunflower leaves, I went back in to create their distinctive serrated edge, using the same shades of thread. If you choose to do the same, simply add extra Straight Stitches overlapping the edges as shown (**fig. 21**), still following the same stitch direction. The leaves can be left as they are, or follow what I did – the creative choice is yours.

## STITCHING THE GREENERY

**13.** For all the assorted sprigs of leaf-like flora, use one or two strands of thread in Long-and-Short Stitch. This particular sprig was filled using green **936** (**fig. 22**). The Colour Guide will suggest which shades to use, but you can also choose your own colour scheme.

**14.** Embroider the stems of the smaller flowers in Split Back Stitch, using three strands of green **936** (**fig. 23**). Follow the curving lines carefully to create the sense of movement all around the hoop.

**15.** Using the same Satin Stitch we used for the larger leaves, fill in the leaves of the decorative flowers using green **469.** Using the same shade of green, embroider the base of the decorative flower heads using Satin Stitch (**fig. 24**).

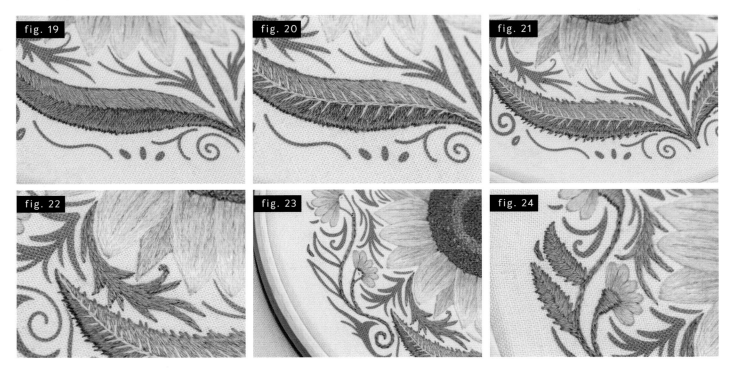

fig. 19  fig. 20  fig. 21  fig. 22  fig. 23  fig. 24

Sunflower

## FINISHING THE DECORATIVE BACKGROUND

**16.** Continue to use the Colour Guide and Photo Guide to help you embroider the background sprigs and swirls of Split Back Stitch (**fig. 25**), clusters of green and yellow Straight Stitches (**fig. 26**) and French Knots (**fig. 27**). Have fun, and always feel free to experiment and use your own colour palette if you wish.

**17.** Outline the five-petal flowers in Split Back Stitch, using two strands of green **833** (**fig. 28**). Fill in the petals using Straight Stitch using two strands of green **833**, referring to the Direction Guide if needed (**fig. 29**). Finish by filling the centre with French Knots in brown **434** (**fig. 30**).

**18.** As a finishing touch to the background, I filled in all the gaps with tiny dispersed Straight Stitches. I used two strands of each colour and followed the curves of the flora to create movement. You can use a single colour throughout, or a range of yellows and greens as I did (**fig. 31**).

That's it! Your sunflower is complete, and I'm sure you gained as much pleasure from embroidering each sunny petal as I have. You will also be well-practised in the art of creating French Knots, so add those to your growing list of stitching skills mastered.

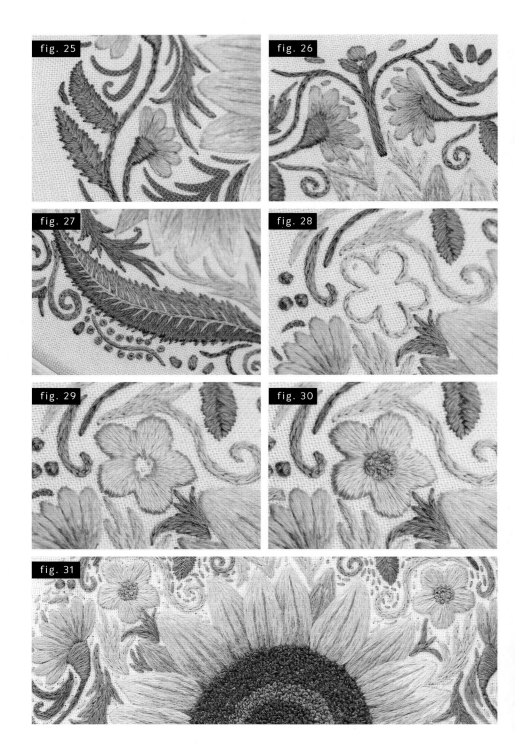

The Projects

Sunflower

# MUSHROOM

## OUR CONNECTION WITH NATURE

*"I'm so glad I live in a world where there are Octobers."*
— **L.M. Montgomery,** *Anne of Green Gables* **(1908)**

Autumn is my favourite season, and what better way to honour it than by embroidering fantastical fungi. The mushroom is widely known and used in cultures all over the world. Rich in tradition and folklore, they are often used for medicine, food and spiritual practice. To me, mushrooms are a symbol of power, abundance, longevity, rebirth, harmony and good luck.

The mushroom's symbiotic connection to the trees and plants around them, representing the circle of life, is a constant reminder to me that we have a connection with everything. There is a magical mycelium network that is abundant, but usually unseen. Mushrooms remind me of the importance of the connection between people and the Earth. My curiosity is always sparked when I spot mushrooms while exploring outside, and whenever I think of autumn, colourful images of fungi are conjured up in my mind.

This embroidery design was inspired by the Boletes mushroom family, of which there are over one-hundred different species. One of my favourite parts of this pattern is the leaves. You can have fun blending the colours, and find joy in how the stitches sit together in contrast to each other. I designed this pattern so that if you don't place your stitches in exactly the same place as me, and the overall effect will still be very much the same. So don't be afraid of embroidering these two mushrooms – there is lots of room for happy mistakes! Feel free to go with the flow and enjoy the repetitive nature of the stitching.

## YOU WILL NEED

### EMBROIDERY COTTON (FLOSS)

A total of 14 skeins of DMC stranded cotton in the following colours. You'll require only one skein of each colour.

- **Browns** 3371 - 938 - 898 - 801
- **Beige** 869 - 167
- **Oranges** 433 - 434 - 300 - 975
- **Greens** 934 - 935 - 936 - 469

### FABRIC

One square no smaller than 30 x 30cm (12 x 12in). I used green linen.

### HOOP

15cm (6in) diameter

### NEEDLE

Size 5–10 embroidery needle (I used Size 10)

### STITCHES USED:

- Long-and-Short Stitch
- Straight Stitch
- Split Back Stitch

See also the Stitch Direction Guide

### STITCHING TIME

Approx. 15–18 hours

### SIZE OF FINISHED EMBROIDERY

Approx. 10.5cm x 8cm (4⅛in x 3⅛in) diameter, displayed in a 15cm (6in) hoop.

## BEFORE YOU BEGIN...

- Transfer the design template onto your fabric as described in Transferring the Patterns, or use the iron-on transfer paper included with the book. With the design placed centrally, mount the fabric in the hoop and tighten the screw as shown.

- If using the colour palette provided (rather than your own), refer to the Colour Guide as you stitch.

- Check the Stitch Direction guide to ensure your stitches are lying correctly.

- Unless specified otherwise, use one strand of cotton (floss) taken from the six divisible strands. See Starting to Stitch for more information.

STITCH DIRECTION

# COLOUR GUIDE

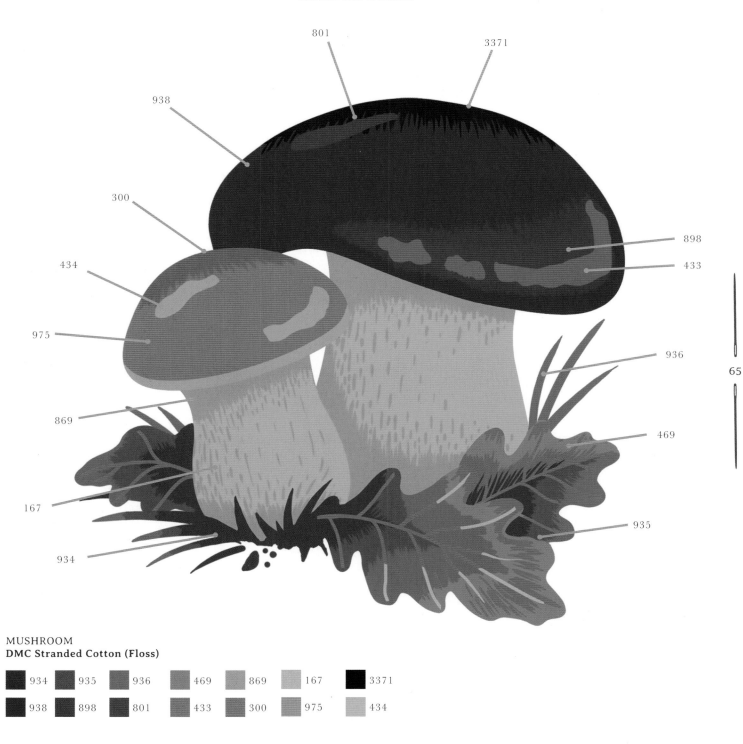

## MUSHROOM
**DMC Stranded Cotton (Floss)**

| | | | | | | | |
|---|---|---|---|---|---|---|---|
| 934 | 935 | 936 | 469 | 869 | 167 | 3371 | |
| 938 | 898 | 801 | 433 | 300 | 975 | 434 | |

Mushroom

66

fig. 1

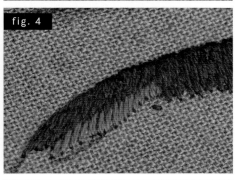

fig. 2

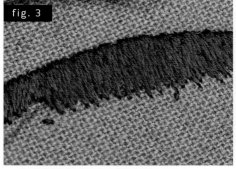

fig. 3

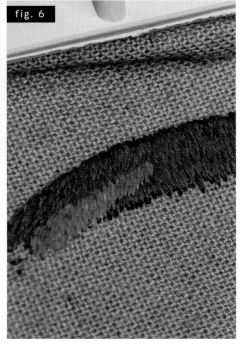

fig. 4

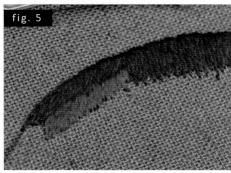

fig. 5

fig. 6

## STITCHING THE LARGE MUSHROOM CAP

**1.** We are beginning with the larger of the two mushrooms. Thread your needle with one or two strands of brown **3371**.

Outline the upper part of the mushroom using Split Back Stitch (**fig. 1**), then begin to fill the area as pictured using Long-and-Short Stitch (**figs. 2 and 3**) . If you're unsure about the exact colour placement, remember to use the Colour Guide as a reference. The mushroom design is very forgiving – if your colour changes don't happen in exactly same place as mine, the overall effect won't be very different.

**2.** Use one strand of brown **801** and Long-and-Short Stitch to create the highlight (**fig. 4**). Then continue using Long-and-Short Stitch in brown **3371** to bring this darkest shade of brown down a little further than we need (**figs. 5 and 6**). Because we are about to blend **3371** into the next colour brown **938**, this technique helps to soften the transition between the two shades.

## TIP

*One strand will result in neater needle-painting, and more subtle and realistic colour graduations. Two strands will have a slightly messier effect, with more obvious contrast between colours.*

67

Mushroom

**3.** Fill in the area as pictured using brown **938** in Long-and-Short Stitch (**fig. 7**). In this case, the contrast between brown **3371** and brown **938** is harsher than I would like (I can't find a reddish brown in the current DMC range to help ease the transition between the two). This may occur often in your needle-painting journey. I have found that the best way to blend these colours in this scenario is to use just one strand of **938** and made some of the longer stitches much longer than I normally would when transitioning between colours. I have found this creates a better of illusion of the colours blending.

**4.** Fill in the next area as pictured using one strand of brown **898** in Long-and-Short Stitch (**fig. 8**). Then, fill the next area using one strand of brown **801** in Long-and-Short Stitch (**fig. 9**), and the next using one strand of orange **433**, again in Long-and-Short Stitch (**fig. 10**).

**5.** Continuing with the same stitch, follow the orange with brown **801**, followed by brown **898** (**Fig. 11**) then finish the cap with brown **938** (**fig. 12**). Fill in the shadowed area of the mushroom with brown **3371** (**fig. 13**).

68

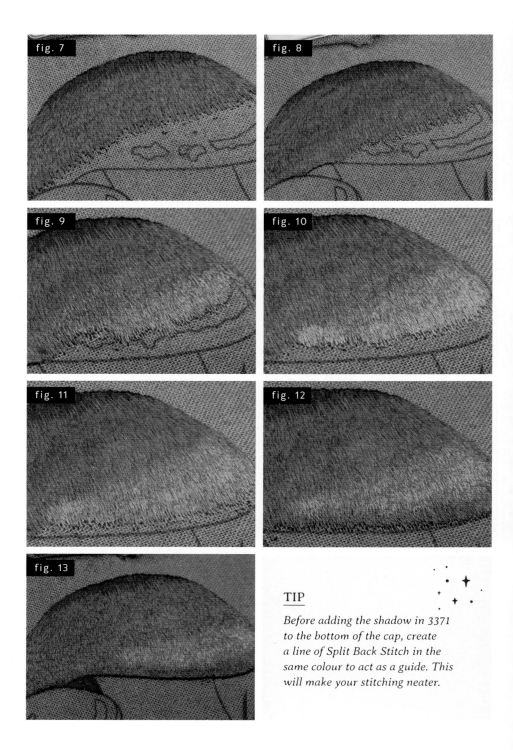

fig. 7

fig. 8

fig. 9

fig. 10

fig. 11

fig. 12

fig. 13

TIP

*Before adding the shadow in 3371 to the bottom of the cap, create a line of Split Back Stitch in the same colour to act as a guide. This will make your stitching neater.*

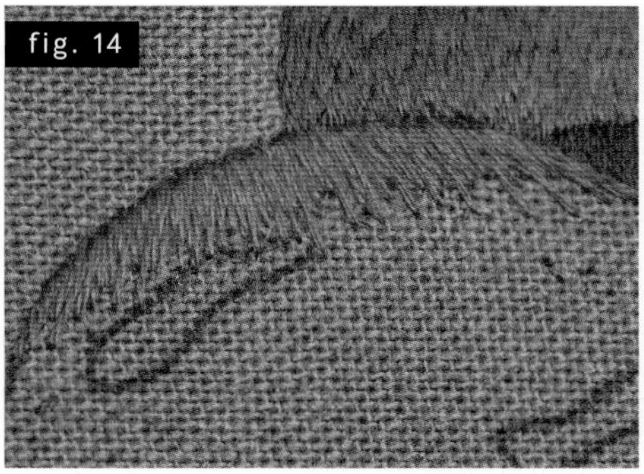

fig. 14

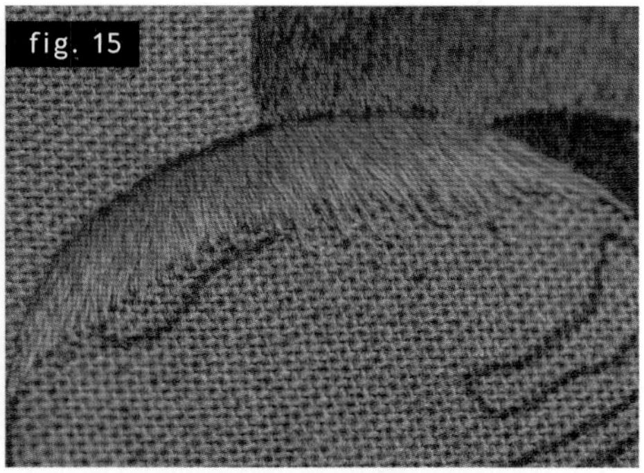

fig. 15

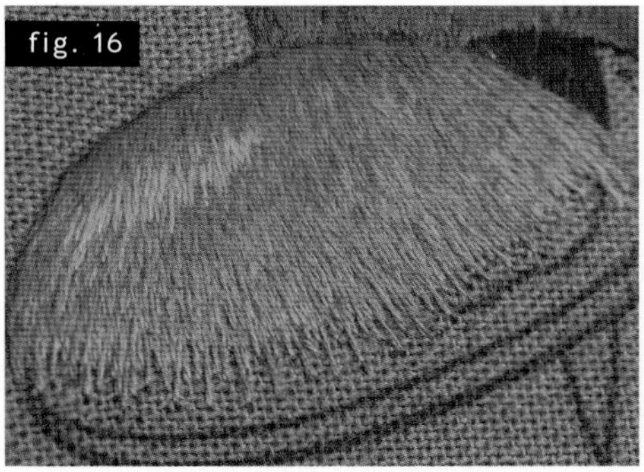

fig. 16

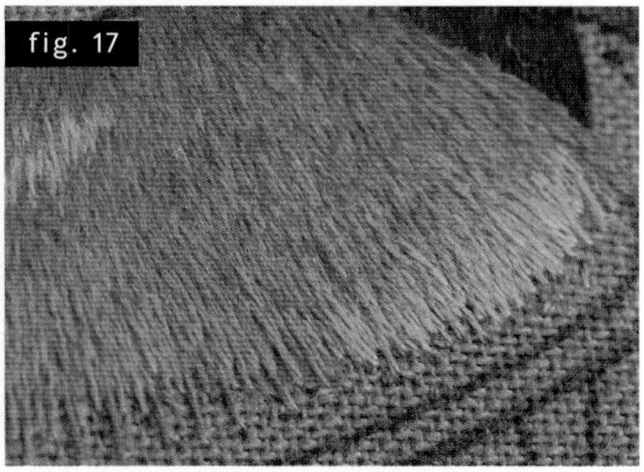

fig. 17

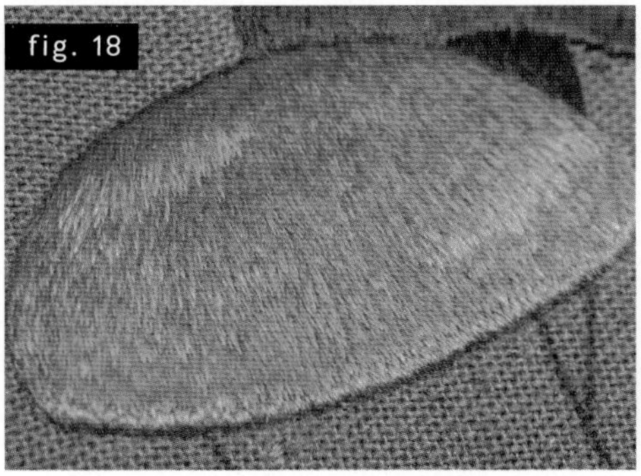

fig. 18

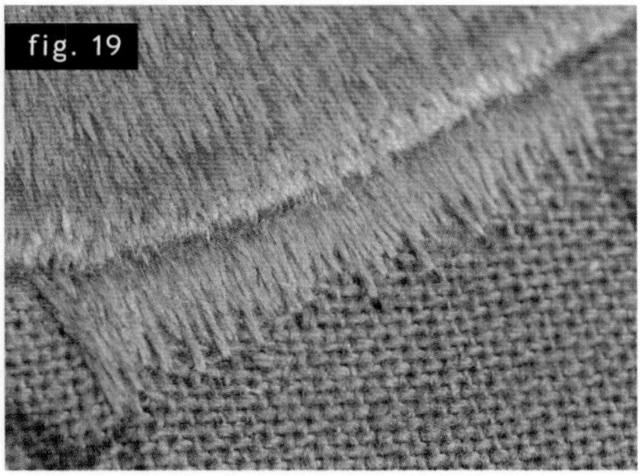

fig. 19

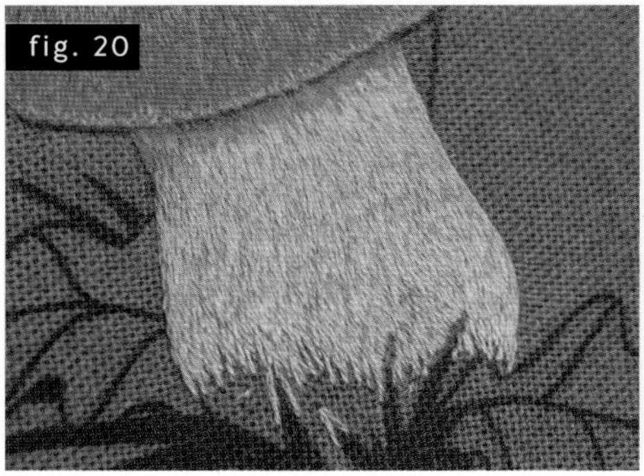

fig. 20

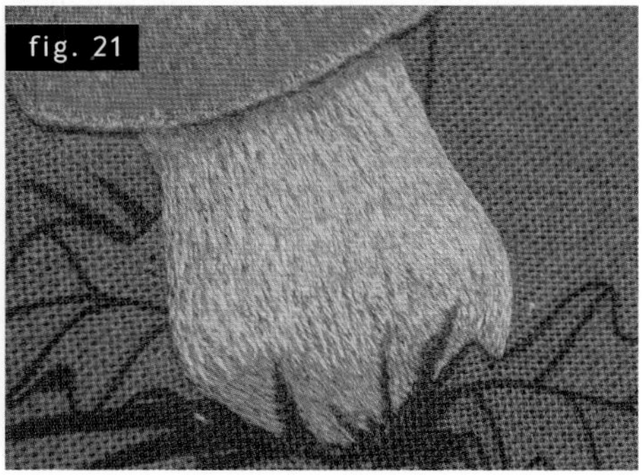

fig. 21

## STITCHING THE SMALL MUSHROOM

**6.** For the second, smaller mushroom, thread your needle with one strand of orange **300** and, as before, outline the top area with Split Back Stitch, then Long-and-Short Stitch (**fig. 14**). Then, change to the lighter shade of orange **975** and continue with Long-and-Short Stitch (**fig. 15**).

**7.** Fill in the first highlight area with orange **434**, then continue filling in with orange **975** (**fig. 16**).

**8.** Fill in the second highlight with orange **434**, followed by orange **975** (**fig. 17**), and then a very small row of orange **434** at the bottom of the mushroom cap (**fig. 18**).

## STITCHING THE STEMS

**9.** Both mushroom stems require only two colours. Begin filling in the smaller mushroom stem using Long-and-Short Stitch with one strand of beige **869** (**fig. 19**).

**10.** Follow the first beige shade with lighter beige **167**, then change back to beige **869** to create a more shadowed effect at the bottom as shown (**fig. 20**). To create more of an illusion of texture and realism, I finished the mushroom stem by adding lots of random straight stitches of beige **869** amongst the **167** (**fig. 21**).

69

Mushroom

**11.** Repeat this process, using Long-and-Short Stitch, for the larger mushroom stem. Begin with beige **869 (fig. 22)**, followed by beige **167**, then beige **869** again **(fig. 23)**. Finish the stem by adding a scattering of Straight Stitches, also in **869 (fig. 24)**. That's the mushrooms finished!

### STITCHING THE FOLIAGE

**12.** Now it's time to stitch the foliage! Begin by filling in the background grass areas using green **936** in Long-and-Short Stitch **(figs. 25 and 26)**.

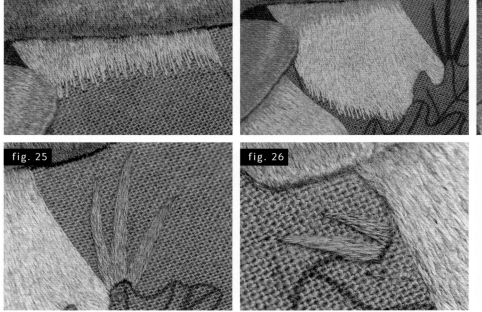

fig. 22

fig. 23

fig. 24

fig. 25

fig. 26

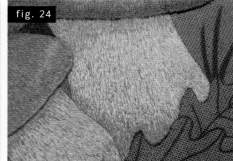

### TIP

*I encourage you to choose your own colour palette, especially with elements such as leaves and flowers, when you can really get creative. The more you practice, the better you will become at choosing your own shades.*

The Projects

**13.** Outline the veins of all three leaves with brown **898 (fig. 27)**. We will be covering these later on so don't worry about making them neat. They are purely there as a guide as the lines tend to get lost as we begin filling in the leaf with shades of green.

**14.** Use Long-and-Short Stitch to begin filling in the upper part of the right-hand leaf with green **936 (fig. 28)**. The stitch direction follows the natural contours of the leaf – see the Stitch Direction guide for more detail. Follow with the lighter shade of green **469 (fig. 29)**. Outline the

edges of the leaf with Split Back Stitch before adding the Long-and-Short Stitch, then place your needle just outside the border of Split Back Stitch for extra neatness.

**15.** After blending green **469** into the darker **936**, I noticed the transition wasn't as smooth as I'd like. To fix this, I picked up one strand of green **936** again. Using my needle to find gaps between the two shades, I added a few longer stitches. This almost creates a second "layer" of stitches (**fig. 30**). As you can see, the result is a smoother colour transition.

**16.** I want the leaf to have more contrast, so we are going to add some straight stitches of green **934** on top of the lighter shade of green **936** in the centre, then begin filling in the lower second half of the leaf with the same shade of green **934 (fig. 31)**.

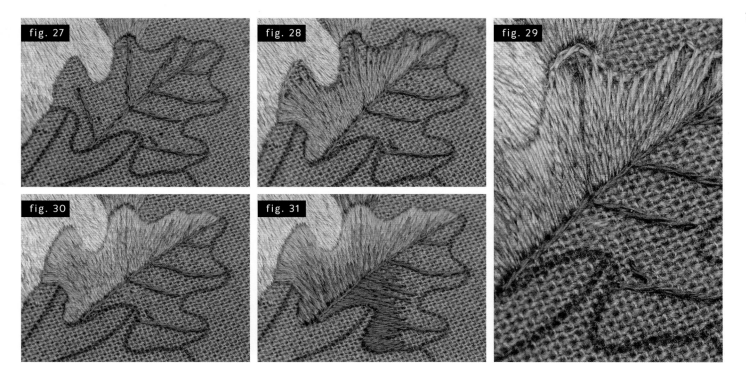

fig. 27

fig. 28

fig. 29

fig. 30

fig. 31

Mushroom

**17.** Follow the green **934** with green **935** and **936** (**figs. 32 and 33**). Then, add just a hint of green **469** with a few random scattered stitches on the outer edge (**fig. 34**).

**18.** Now we move on to the left-hand leaf. As before, fill in the veins with brown **898** using Split Back Stitch. Then begin filling in the leaf as pictured. Begin with green 934, then **935** (**fig. 35**), and ending with **936** at the edges (**fig. 36**).

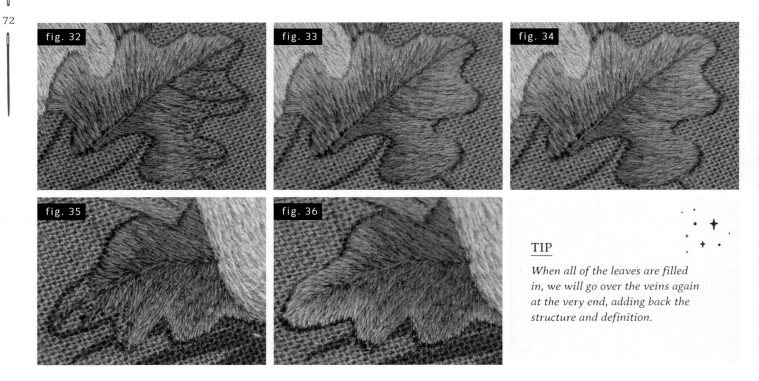

fig. 32

fig. 33

fig. 34

fig. 35

fig. 36

### TIP

*When all of the leaves are filled in, we will go over the veins again at the very end, adding back the structure and definition.*

72

The Projects

**19.** Now let's begin the largest oak leaf at the front of the design. Fill in the veins using brown **898** in Split Back Stitch. Then begin filling in the leaf as pictured, transitioning from the darkest shade of green **934**, then **935** (**fig. 37**). Begin filing in the leaf with green **936** (**fig. 38**).

**20**. It's time to add a brighter highlight to the leaf, resulting in a nice contrast that is pleasing to the eye. Use green **469** as pictured, working in Long-and-Short Stitch (**fig. 39**).

**21**. Oak leaves are lovely when they begin to transition to those warm brown shades in the autumn. To reflect this, add in beige **869** as pictured, using Long-and-Short Stitch (**fig. 40**). As you can see, I added in a few Straight Stitches of **869** amongst the previously stitched green as well. This helps create balance and the illusion of blending that you would use with paint, but in this case, it is scattered straight stitches of embroidery thread. Use green **936** to finish this section of the leaf (**fig. 41**).

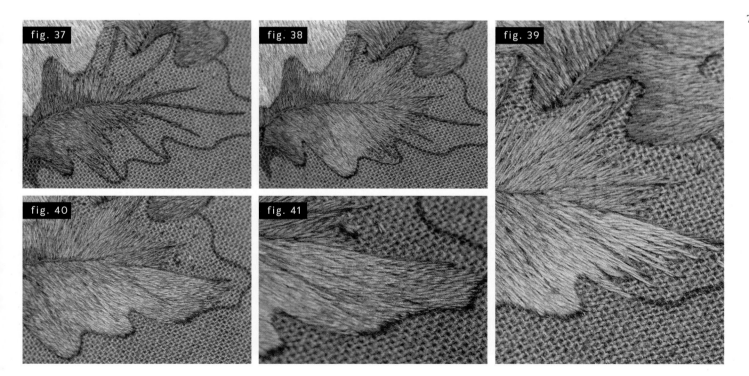

fig. 37

fig. 38

fig. 39

fig. 40

fig. 41

Mushroom

**22.** For the upper part of this leaf, begin stitching with green **469** (**fig. 42**), then transition to beige **869**, and back to **469** as pictured (**fig. 43**).

**23.** To finish all of the leaves, use Split Back Stitch to redefine the veins in beige **869** (**fig. 44**). For the largest leaf, I extended some of the veins with the lighter shade of beige **167** (**fig. 45**). I also added a few more random stitches of beige **869** amongst the rest of the leaves at this point, adding colour balance to the overall piece (**fig. 46**).

**24.** Use Long-and-Short Stitch to fill in the front section of grass in the shade green **934** (**fig. 47**). You can follow the same stitch direction as I did (see the Stitch Direction diagram), or make it a little more random. Add in extra blades of grass if you wish.

**25.** Finish the final section of grass, blending from green **934**, to **935** to **936** (**figs. 48 and 49**). You have now completed your mushrooms – congratulations!

Finally, your mushroom is finished! Now you can stand back and enjoy the results of time well spent. With such warm autumnal shades and detailed leaves, your latest hoop will draw many admiring glances.

74

The Projects

Mushroom

# ROBIN

*"The robin flew from his swinging spray of ivy on to the top of the wall and he opened his beak and sang a loud, lovely trill, merely to show off. Nothing in the world is quite as adorably lovely as a robin when he shows off – and they are nearly always doing it."* — **Frances Hodgson Burnett**, *The Secret Garden* (1911)

It had been a few years since I'd designed a bird, so this robin was a breath of fresh air. To me, the robin symbolizes our budding relationship with the natural world. Even in an urban environment, spotting a robin always reminds me that wildlife is closer than we think – we just have to know where to look. Each time I embroider an animal, I feel like I am honouring in it some way – the time it takes studying them to learn their subtle differences. Most of us think of robins as having a red breast, but upon observing them, both in photos and on my bird feeder, I learnt that their breast is a variety of vibrant oranges. I couldn't wait to choose the shades of cotton (floss) to reflect this mesmerizing beauty.

When considering the flora and fauna, I wanted the design to be interchangeable for the seasons. To make the hoop more festive, it would be easy to embroider red berries instead of the fluffy brown flora I chose. You could also select fabric in a colour that would really suit your home – I've made some suggestions in the project. Personally, I want to hang this hoop in my home all year round, hence the neutral colour choices I made. I also didn't want you to have to purchase too many shades of floss; using colours in the background that I had already used for the robin was both a creative and thrifty decision!

## YOU WILL NEED

### EMBROIDERY COTTON (FLOSS)

A total of 18 skeins of DMC stranded cotton in the following colours. You'll require only one skein of each colour.

- **Cream** 738
- **Yellows** 783 - 3045
- **Oranges** 976 - 301 - 167
- **Browns** 801 - 400 - 3371 - 3031 - 3781 - 3862 - 3790 - 3032
- **White** 3865
- **Greens** 3011 - 3012
- **Black** 310

### FABRIC

One square no smaller than 30 x 30cm (12 x 12in). I used organic unbleached cotton calico.

### HOOP

15cm (6in) diameter

### NEEDLE

Size 5–10 embroidery needle (I used Size 10)

### STITCHES USED:

- Long-and-Short Stitch
- French Knot
- Straight Stitch
- Split Back Stitch

See also the Stitch Direction Guide

### STITCHING TIME

Approx. 18–22 hours

### SIZE OF FINISHED EMBROIDERY

Approx. 14.2cm (5¾in) diameter, displayed in a 15cm (6in) hoop. The robin alone measures approx. 8 x 7cm (3¼ x 2 ¾in)

## BEFORE YOU BEGIN...

- Transfer the design template onto your fabric as described in Transferring the Patterns, or use the iron-on transfer paper included with the book. With the design placed centrally, mount the fabric in the hoop and tighten the screw as shown.

- If using the colour palette provided (rather than your own), refer to the Colour Guide as you stitch.

- Check the Stitch Direction guide to ensure your stitches are lying correctly.

- Unless specified otherwise, use one strand of cotton (floss) taken from the six divisible strands. See Starting to Stitch for more information.

STITCH DIRECTION

ROBIN
**DMC Stranded Cotton (Floss)**

| | | | | | | | | |
|---|---|---|---|---|---|---|---|---|
| 3865 | 310 | 3371 | 3031 | 801 | 3862 | 3790 | 3032 | 167 |
| 3045 | 738 | 783 | 976 | 301 | 400 | 3781 | 3011 | 3012 |

Robin

80

## STITCHING THE FACE AND CHEST

**1.** Begin with the eye of the robin. Thread your needle with one strand of black **310** and outline the eye using Split Back Stitch. Try to keep your stitches as tiny as possible as this will ensure a smoother circle. **(fig. 1)**.

**2.** Still using one strand of black **310**, fill in the eye using Satin Stitch **(fig. 2)**. Leave a gap to create the reflection of the eye. Use one strand of **3865** for the reflection of the eye using Split Back Stitch. If you find

the white is getting lost in the black of the eye, stitch a second layer of white over the top of the previously stitched reflection to make it more prominent **(fig. 3)**.

**3.** With the eye complete, it's time to start on the beak. Use brown **3031** and a mix of Long-and-Short Stitch and Straight Stitch to fill in the beak as pictured **(fig. 4)**.

**4.** Fill in the smaller gap as pictured using brown **801 (fig. 5)**. If you're unsure about colour placement, you can refer to the Colour Guide at any time. Then fill in the larger area of the beak using brown **3862 (fig. 6)**.

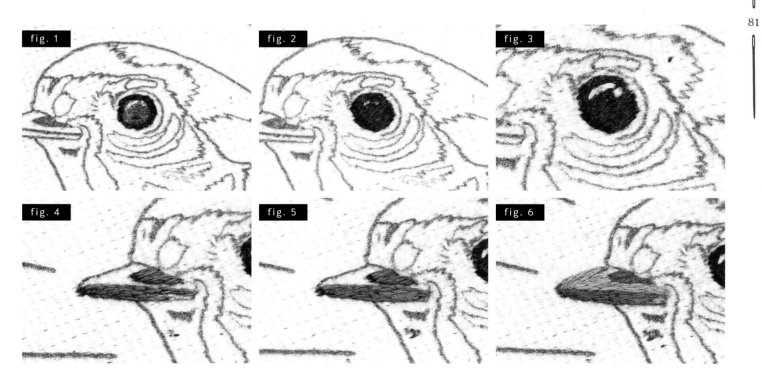

fig. 1

fig. 2

fig. 3

fig. 4

fig. 5

fig. 6

Robin

**5.** To finish the beak, fill in the remaining area using Long-and-Short Stitch in brown **3790**.

Moving on to the head, begin filling the area around the beak with the lightest shade of yellow, **783**, as shown on the Colour Guide **(fig. 7)**. Using the same colour, outline the eye in Split Back Stitch to keep things neat and ensure you are less likely to stitch over the black stitches later on.

**6.** Now begin filling in the feathers of the head and chest, starting with orange **976** and Long-and-Short Stitch to build up the texture **(Fig. 8)**. Use yellow **783** and the same stitch to form a curve around the contour of the eye **(fig. 9)**. Fill in the next area of the chest with orange **976** as pictured **(fig. 10)**.

**7.** Using Long-and-Short Stitch, continue to work back from the chest and across the face. Use the Colour Guide and template outlines to help you select and place the colours. Begin by adding Long-and-Short Stitches around the eye and down the chest in orange **301**, paying attention to the Stitch Direction guide **(fig. 11)**.

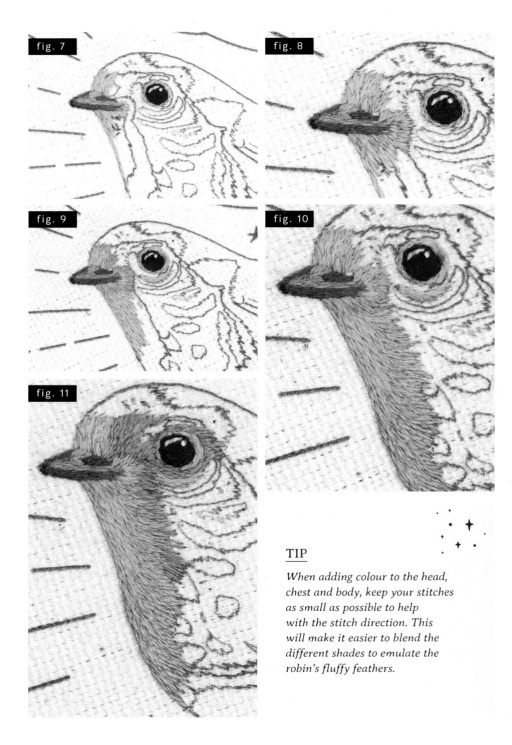

fig. 7

fig. 8

fig. 9

fig. 10

fig. 11

### TIP

*When adding colour to the head, chest and body, keep your stitches as small as possible to help with the stitch direction. This will make it easier to blend the different shades to emulate the robin's fluffy feathers.*

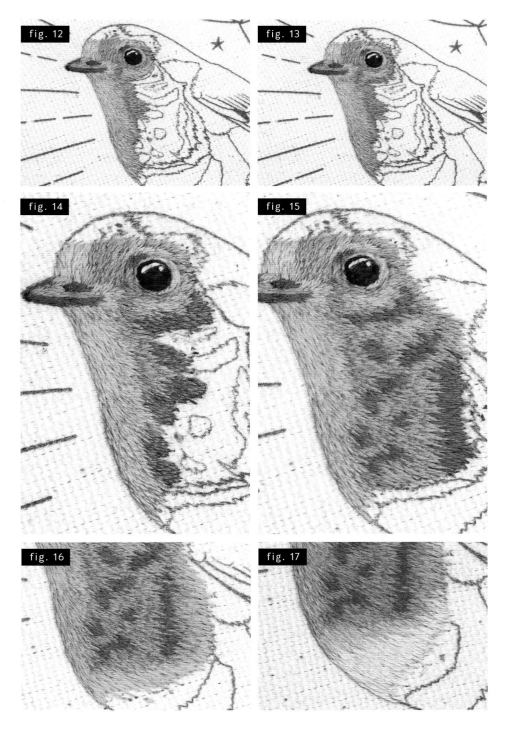

fig. 12

fig. 13

fig. 14

fig. 15

fig. 16

fig. 17

**8.** Continue to work small Long-and-Short Stitches around the eye, following the Colour Guide and Stitch Direction guide carefully. Adding brown **400** in the space above the eye starts to build depth **(fig. 12)** then angle your stitches outwards as you start to fill the rest of the face **(fig. 13)**.

**9.** The next few stages will reveal the markings that create the texture across the robin's chest. Carry on using Long-and-Short Stitch, blending brown **400** into the previously stitched orange **301** **(fig. 14)**. Continue in this way, blending the two colours along their edges, working backwards towards the wing **(fig. 15)**.

**10.** The robin's distinctive rust coloured chest now fades into yellow and cream. Begin with yellow **783** **(fig. 16)**, blending it into cream **738 (fig. 17)**. Your Long-and-Short Stitch will comprise mainly of longer stitches as the colour begins to sweep towards the robin's underside.

83

Robin

## STITCHING THE HEAD AND BODY

**11.** Using Long-and-Short Stitch, begin blending brown **3790** at the top of the robin's head (**fig. 18**), followed by brown **3862** (**fig. 19**).

**12.** Continuing to use Long-and-Short Stitch, blend yellow **3045** into the previously stitched cream **738** (**fig. 20**). Follow this with brown **3032** (**fig. 21**).

**13.** To complete filling in the body, use the same stitch to fill in the next area using orange **167** (**fig. 22**), followed by yellow **3045** (**fig. 23**).

**14.** Now that you've finished filling in the areas of the body with their colours, you may find that you would like to blend those colours together where they meet. To create this effect, overlay the colours using sparse, scattered Straight Stitches.

84

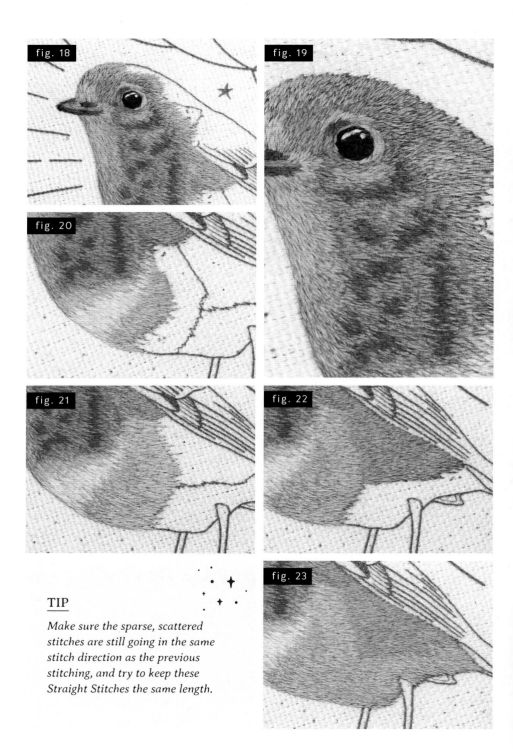

fig. 18

fig. 19

fig. 20

fig. 21

fig. 22

fig. 23

### TIP

*Make sure the sparse, scattered stitches are still going in the same stitch direction as the previous stitching, and try to keep these Straight Stitches the same length.*

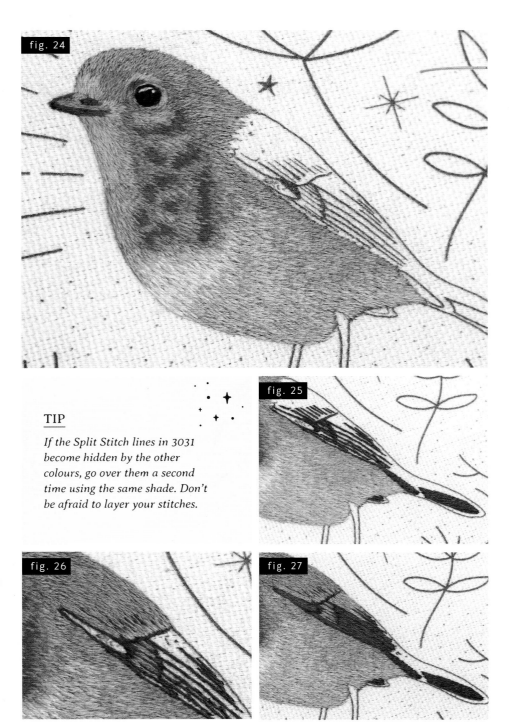

For example, in the previous step, in the area where we stitched with orange **167**, use one strand of yellow **3045** to add a few Straight Stitches close to where these two colours meet. Then do the opposite, threading your needle with one strand of orange **167** and add a few scattered stitches amongst yellow **3045** in the area close to where the two colours meet (**fig. 24**). I have illustrated this in the Colour Guide for all areas of the robin to help further with placement.

### STITCHING THE WING AND LEGS

**15**. Outline and colour in all the areas of the wing that use brown **3031**, as indicated on the Colour Guide. Use Split Back Stitch for the outlines, and Long-and-Short Stitch for filling (**fig. 25**).

**16**. Still using Long-and-Short Stitch, begin filling in the areas on the Colour Guide that use brown **3862** and yellow **3045** as shown (**fig. 26**). In the same way, fill in the areas that use yellow **3045** and brown **801** as shown (**fig. 27**).

fig. 24

fig. 25

fig. 26

fig. 27

### TIP

*If the Split Stitch lines in 3031 become hidden by the other colours, go over them a second time using the same shade. Don't be afraid to layer your stitches.*

Robin

17. Finish filling in the rest of the wing, using Long-and-Short Stitch in brown **3862**. To add further definition to the wing, use the same colour to add lines of Split Back Stitch next to the previously stitched brown **3031** outlines (**fig. 28**). This will help the outlines to 'pop', as the brown **801** partly hid the definition created by the Split Back Stitch in the previous step. To add more texture to the feathers around the robin's belly and upper back, I also added some sparse Straight Stitches in brown **801** (**fig. 29**).

18. Moving on to the legs, use Split Back Stitch in brown **801** to outline the front of the legs and toes (**Fig. 30**), then use the same colour to fill them in with Long-and-Short Stitch (**fig. 31**). Continue to fill in the legs and define the claws using brown **3862** and **3031**. Keep your stitches small and follow the natural curve of the legs and claws. It doesn't matter too much if you don't place the browns exactly as I have – you will achieve the same overall effect (**fig. 32**).

86

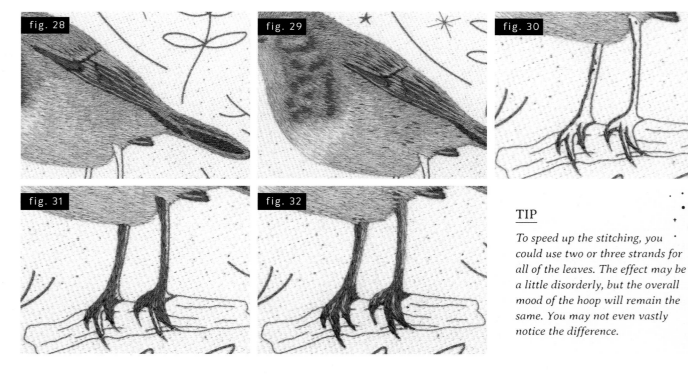

fig. 28

fig. 29

fig. 30

fig. 31

fig. 32

### TIP

*To speed up the stitching, you could use two or three strands for all of the leaves. The effect may be a little disorderly, but the overall mood of the hoop will remain the same. You may not even vastly notice the difference.*

## STITCHING THE BRANCH

**19**. With the robin complete, we can fill in the branch. To begin, define the texture of the bark, using Straight Stitch in brown **3371 (fig. 33)**. Then use brown **3781** to fill it with colour **(fig. 34)**. Using two contrasting shades of brown, rather than only one, adds subtle realism to the branch Because we didn't outline the branch before filling it in, the stitches on either end give the wood a ragged, organic look.

**20**. Finish the branch by making French Knots using greens **3011** and **3012 (fig. 35)**. The resulting stitches will look like tiny pieces of moss growing on the bark, while using two different shades of green adds to the material effect. For my French Knots, I used two strands of cotton (floss) and wrapped my needle with the thread twice.

## STITCHING THE FOLIAGE

**21**. With our centrepiece complete, we can eagerly begin the foliage! Start by filling in all the branches using brown **3862 (fig. 36)**. I used three strands of cotton (floss) in Split Back Stitch.

**22**. Fill in the sprigs of green leaves using Split Back Stitch in green **3011** for the stems (again, I used three strands) **(fig. 37)**. Then fill in the leaves using Long-and-Short Stitch. I filled half of each leaf with green **3011**, and half with green **3012 (fig. 38)**. Use one strand for the smaller leaves, and two strands for the larger leaves. I like the split effect of the two greens on the leaves (the placement of light and dark on each leaf adds realistic dimension, as if the paler parts are catching the light), but feel free to experiment and do with them as you wish. I always encourage creative freedom, so don't be afraid to follow your own vision!

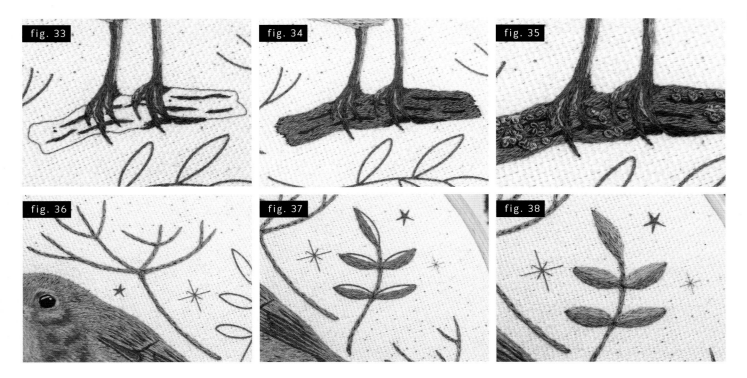

fig. 33

fig. 34

fig. 35

fig. 36

fig. 37

fig. 38

Robin

**23.** At the top of the brown branches, begin to stitch the fluffy star-like flowers. I used three strands of yellow **3045**. To create the stitch, first create four lines pointing north, south, east and west, radiating from the centre point (try to leave a little gap in the middle as shown). Then between the four lines, stitch another four, again leaving space in the middle. Repeat for a third time if desired, stitching a further eight lines, to create the starburst effect with the middle defined by negative space **(fig. 39)**.

For the neatest results, try to keep the lines created at each stage of even length, resulting in a rounded, symmetrical shape. However, it really doesn't matter if they aren't perfect – improvise and experiment with styles and sizes as I have **(fig. 40)**!

### STITCHING THE STARS

**24.** For the simple eight-pointed stars, use one strand of brown **3862** and follow the lines using a straight stitch so that each one crosses at the centre **(fig. 41)**.

**25.** I decided it would be more aesthetically pleasing for the eight points to widen towards the centre of the star, creating a slightly tapered effect towards each point. I achieved this by embroidering a second and third layer of straight stitches, decreasing onto the star.

To do the same, bring your needle up halfway through one of the eight lines radiating from the centre, then back down through the halfway point on the opposite side of the centre. Repeat this step by bringing the needle up, then down, moving closer to the centre two or three times on each line until you are happy with how it looks **(fig. 42)**! The stars are fun to embroider and if you make a mistake and the line isn't straight enough for your liking, it is easy to undo.

fig. 39

fig. 40

fig. 41

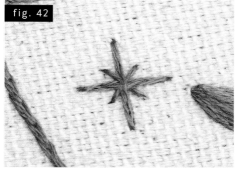

fig. 42

fig. 43

fig. 44

fig. 45

**26**. Fill in the denser, five-pointed stars using one strand of brown **801**. I did this by bringing my needle up at each point of the star and down through the centre, working my way round to cover all of the transferred pattern **(fig. 43)**. I wasn't worried about making this precise or neat – the goal was simply to fill the star. The dark shade used disguises irregularities in the stitching, and admirers of your embroidery aren't going to be closely analyzing your little stars. The overall effect is what matters here!

**27**. To build up the background of the hoop a little, I added a variety of French Knots in different sizes using yellow **3045 (fig. 44)**. To create different sizes, I experiment with using more or fewer strands of cotton (floss). No matter how many strands I use, I like to wrap the needle only twice, as this results in fewer tangles and neater knots.

**28**. The final stage is to stitch the sunburst effect emanating from our little friend – it almost emulates the feeling of birdsong! You will have already added the French Knots in the previous step, so now use two strands of brown **3862** to fill in the solid lines with Chain Stitch, and two strands of the darker brown **801** for the Straight Stitch dashed lines **(fig. 45)**.

And voilà – you've finished your robin hoop! This was a challenging embroidery, so congratulations friend! Take great pride and satisfaction in your stitching. We are all our own worst critics, so don't worry if your finished piece isn't as "perfect" as you might want it to be. Life is about the journey, not the destination. It's tempting to focus on the flaws, but you can use them to see how you can improve next time. Take everything you learnt from this embroidery into your next creation! I'm beyond sure your embroidered robin is beautiful.

89

## TIP

*You could replace the background French Knots with the swirling Straight Stitches used elsewhere in the book. However for me, a sprinkling of French Knots captures the magical atmosphere of a robin close-by.*

Robin

# HONEY BEE

## OUR SPELLBINDING FRIEND

**The natural world always inspires us, providing moments to self-reflect. So what better way to sum up the seasons than to honour the honey bee - the fascinating little creature that busies itself all year round. To me, the honey bee is a symbol of community, hard work, creation and feminine power.**

This embroidery design is the most intricate pattern in the book; the wide array of colours and tiny details take a long time to embroider. However, it is also one of the most rewarding to complete. After a lot of love, patience and delayed gratification, you'll be holding your creation with a great sense of achievement. Mounted in a simple hoop, you'll be proud to hang it in your home or gift it to a loved one.

I've designed this to be a versatile addition to your pattern library; you can embroider the honey bee only, omitting the floral background for a quicker but no less stunning result. Or choose your own colour palette for the background – match it to the decor of your home or the colours in your garden. You could even use a single colour, such as white on white. (You may already be familiar with this tactile technique, often referred to as whitework or Mountmellick.) Whichever path you choose, the repetitive, meditative motion of the stitching will take you into your own magical world.

As always, there are lots of tips to help you with the pattern, and detailed photos showing my own progress as I stitched the honey bee and flora. Whether you're stitching outside in nature or snuggled up at home with a movie, you've got this, my stitching friends!

## YOU WILL NEED

**EMBROIDERY COTTON (FLOSS)**

A total of 19 skeins of DMC stranded cotton in the following colours. You'll require only one skein of each colour. Colours marked* use the same skein for both the flora and the honey bee.

*Flora*

- **Greens** 730 - 371 - 610 - 612 - 935
- **Yellows** 782* - 434
- **Browns** 801* - 3371*
- **Pinks** 3802 - 3722
- **White** 3865*

*Honey bee*

- **Black** 310
- **White** 3865
- **Browns** 3371 - 801 - 3031 - 3862 - 3863 - 3864
- **Yellows** 420 - 782 - 422

**FABRIC**

One square no smaller than 30 x 30cm (12 x 12in)

**HOOP**

15cm (6in) diameter

**NEEDLE**

Size 5–10 embroidery needle (I used Size 10)

**STITCHES USED:**

- Long-and-Short Stitch
- Straight Stitch
- Split Back Stitch
- Satin Stitch
- French Knot

See also the Stitch Direction Guide

**STITCHING TIME**

Approx. 20–24 hours

**SIZE OF FINISHED EMBROIDERY**

Approx. 14.8cm (5⅞in) diameter, displayed in a 15cm (6in) hoop. The bee on its own measures approx. 8.2 x 7.2cm (3¼ x 3¾in)

## BEFORE YOU BEGIN...

- Transfer the design template onto your fabric as described in Transferring the Patterns, or use the iron-on transfer paper included with the book. With the design placed centrally, mount the fabric in the hoop and tighten the screw as shown.

- If using the colour palette provided (rather than your own), refer to the Colour Guide as you stitch.

- Check the Stitch Direction guide to ensure your stitches are lying correctly.

- Unless specified otherwise, use one strand of cotton (floss) taken from the six divisible strands. See Starting to Stitch for more information.

STITCH DIRECTION

# COLOUR GUIDE

3865

3722

782

612

310

434

3862

3863

3864

801

371

610

730

3371

420

3031

935

3802

422

93

Honey Bee

## HONEY BEE

| | | | | | |
|---|---|---|---|---|---|
| 310 | 3865 | 3371 | 801 | 3031 | 3862 |
| 3863 | 3864 | 420 | 782 | 422 | |

94

## STITCHING THE FLORA

**1.** We begin with the flora on the lower left of the design. Thread your needle with two strands of green **730** and prepare to stitch (see Starting to Stitch). Using Split Back Stitch, follow the outline of the stems **(fig. 1)**.

**2.** Now thread your needle with just one strand of **730**. Use Split Back Stitch to complete the smaller parts of each stem's upper section, and to outline the larger leaves as shown **(fig. 2)**.

**3.** Still using one strand of **730**, fill in the small leaves using Long-and-Short Stitch. Being so small, these leaves can be tricky to fill, so be forgiving with yourself if every stitch is not picture-perfect – enjoy the process. Fill in the remaining leaves with green **371** using Long-and-Short Stitch **(fig. 3)**.

**4.** Use two strands of yellow **434** to create the French Knots for the flowers at the top of the larger stems. Following the Stitch Guide, I wrapped the thread around my needle twice to create a dense but delicate little bud effect **(figs. 4 and 5)**.

You can see how I "draw" an outline first **(fig. 4)** to make it easier to evenly fill the space.

### TIP

*If you want your buds to be bigger and fluffier than mine, you can experiment with using three or four strands of floss instead of two.*

**5.** As I find it easier to work on one colour palette at a time, I went on to complete the flora that was similar throughout the design, in this case at 11 o'clock **(fig. 6)** and 3 o'clock.

95

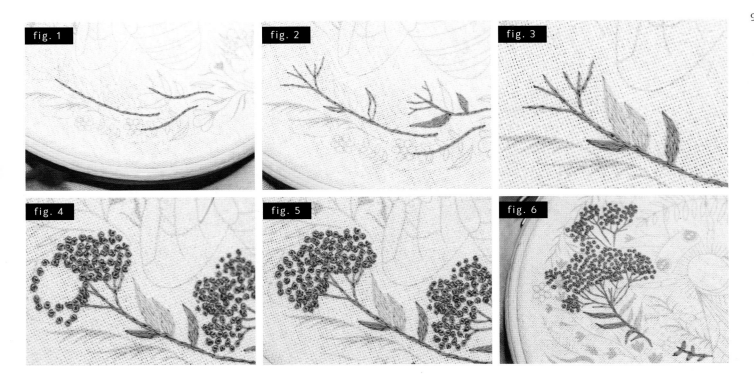

fig. 1    fig. 2    fig. 3
fig. 4    fig. 5    fig. 6

Honey Bee

**6.** For the daisy stems, use two strands of green **730**, and for the leaves one strand of **730**. Due to their small nature, the leaves are a combination of straight stitches (**fig. 7**), rather than the flowing nature of Long-and-Short Stitch, which is more suited to larger surface areas.

**7.** Outline the daisy petals with one strand of white **3865**, using Split Back Stitch (**fig. 8**). Then fill in using straight stitches (**fig. 9**). I achieved the neatest result by bringing the needle up on the outside of the daisy, just next to the Split Back Stitch, then pushing it down through the centre of the flower.

To complete the daisies, use two strands of yellow **782** to fill the centre with French Knots (**fig. 10**). Repeat this process for all seven daisies.

**8.** It's now time to start the fern-like plant on the immediate right side of the honey bee. Using two strands of green **935**, fill in the stem with Split Back Stitch (**fig. 11**). To create the gradient effect on the leaves, use Long-and-Short Stitch to fill them in. Begin with **935**, starting from the centre outwards to fill the inner half of the leaves (**fig. 12**). Then change to the lighter green of **730** and fill in the outer half of the leaves (**fig. 13**).

96

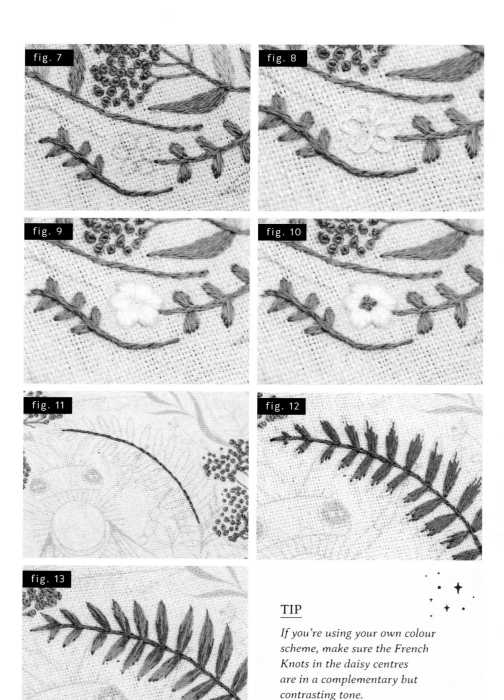

## TIP

*If you're using your own colour scheme, make sure the French Knots in the daisy centres are in a complementary but contrasting tone.*

fig. 14

fig. 15

fig. 16

fig. 17

fig. 18

fig. 19

**9**. Using the Colour Guide, you can now begin to fill in the remaining areas of the floral background using combinations of straight stitch, Split Back Stitch, and Long-and-Short Stitch.

For ease of stitching, I work on one colour at a time. In this case, I selected green **935** first, locating all the areas of the design using this colour. I went on to fill all those section at once, before moving onto the next shade, and so on (**fig. 14**).

**10**. For the yellow flowers, use one strand of yellow **782** to Split Back Stitch the outline (**fig. 15**), then use Long-and-Short Stitch to fill it in. If you'd like to create a bit more depth, you can add a little bit of yellow **434** as I did (**fig. 16**). At the base of the flower, use green **730** to create a tiny Satin Stitch. I think it finishes off the flower nicely.

Continue to embroider the remaining yellow flowers, their stems and leaves. Use the Colour Guide to fill in the areas as pictured (**fig. 17**), (**fig. 18**) and (**fig. 19**).

## TIP

*If the colours aren't placed exactly where I put them, that's fine. I highly encourage you to choose your own creative vision for colour placement and have fun.*

Honey Bee

**11.** Before stitching the two large pink flowers, start with their leaves to create realistic depth using green **730**, **371** and **935**. Angle straight stitches slightly downwards towards the centre of the leaf. I find it easier to begin at the bottom of the leaf and work my way upwards. Complete the leaves by using one strand of **935** for the centre veins **(fig. 20)**.

**12.** Outline the flower in Split Back Stitch, using one strand of pink **3722** **(fig. 21)**, then use Long-and-Short Stitch to fill in the petals as pictured **(fig. 22)**. Create a gradient from pink **3722** to **3802**, then use two strands of yellow **782** to finish with a centre of French Knots **(fig. 23)**. Repeat this step for the pink flower and leaves at 12 o'clock.

**13.** As a finishing touch to the background, I filled in all the gaps with tiny dispersed Straight Stitches. I used two strands of each colour and followed the curves of the flora to create movement.

You can either use a single colour throughout, or a range of colours as I did. I created a gradient by moving from dark to light e.g. using shades of green starting with **935**, and moving through **730**, **371** and so on **(fig. 24)**. I also gradually moved between colours e.g. allowing green to flow into brown **(fig. 25)**.

98

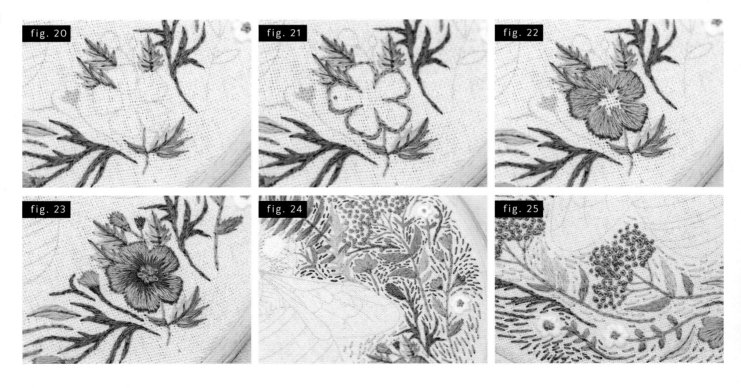

fig. 20  fig. 21  fig. 22
fig. 23  fig. 24  fig. 25

When filling space around the larger flora, such as the pink flowers, I allowed the colour of the petals to 'pop' by using a lighter shade of green around them **(fig. 26)**.

14. You should have now completed the background **(fig. 27)**, and your stitching will look something like this. Check over your stitching for forgotten areas or gaps. In the next stage, we'll move onto the honey bee.

## STITCHING THE HONEY BEE
### The head

15. We'll start with the eyes. Humans are instinctively drawn to the eyes of any face – even of the tiniest creature – so it's important to make them symmetrical and engaging. The two white dots of light emphasize the appeal, a technique often used in animé, but I toned it down to retain realism.

To begin, outline the eyes and top of the head in Split Back Stitch, using black **310 (fig. 28)**.

16. Then, use tiny stitches to fill in the eyes. The area is small so a bit tricky; I positioned my needle on the outside of the Split Back Stitch, then filled in the eyes with a mixture of Satin Stitch and Straight Stitch. Then use one strand of white **3865** to create the light reflected in and around the eyes **(fig. 29)**.

This bit can be a little tricky, but you can always undo the stitches and try again if you're not happy. Embroidery is always very forgiving.

fig. 26

fig. 27

fig. 28

fig. 29

## TIP

*By stitching the outline of the eyes first, you have a chance to correct any errors, easily unpicking those stitches without disturbing surrounding embroidery.*

Honey Bee

**17.** Use vertical Long-and-Short Stitch to fill in the shades of the head. Graduate from black **310** (**fig. 30**) through brown **3371**, **801** and yellow **420**. Before you reach the final row, Split Back Stitch the antennae using brown **3031** (**fig. 31**). The final row – yellow **782** – doesn't need to be a full, dense row. Instead, intermittently disperse the stitches to add a highlight of saturated yellow (**fig. 32**).

### The thorax

**18.** With the head completed, we move onto the next section of the honey bee – the thorax. Use one strand of brown **3371** to fill in the lower curved area using Split Back Stitch (**fig. 33**).

Then starting from the lower edge and working upwards, fill the main part of the thorax in the following shade order: brown **801**, **3031** (**fig. 34**), **3862** and **3031** (**fig. 35**). Angle your stitches slightly outward to create a more natural effect.

**19.** Still angling your stitches outwards, add the outer row of brown **3371**, and scatter some random stitches of brown **801** above the initial row of **801** as shown (**fig. 36**).

**20.** Fill in the tiny crescent shape, using brown **3864**, **3031** and yellow **420** (**fig. 37**). Angle your stitches more horizontally and follow the curve of the outline.

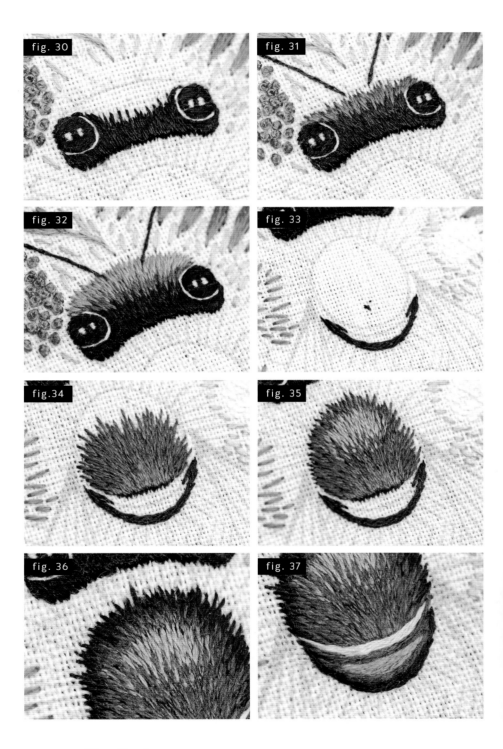

fig. 30 fig. 31 fig. 32 fig. 33 fig.34 fig. 35 fig. 36 fig. 37

The Projects

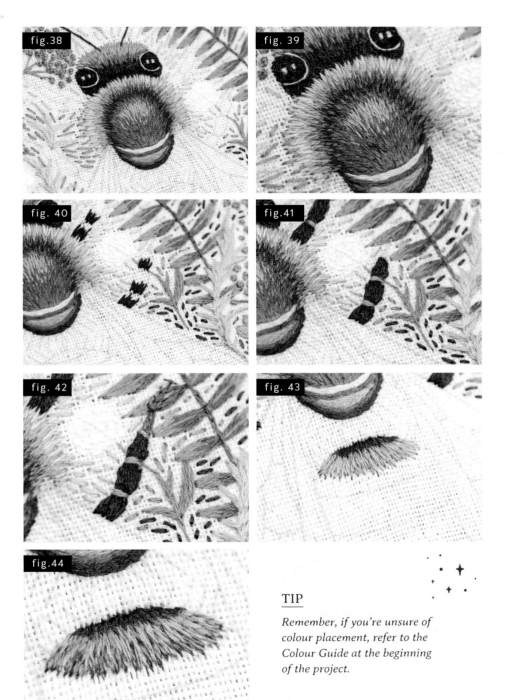

**21.** To finish the fluffy thorax, graduate from the previously stitched brown **3371**, to the brown **801**, yellow **420** then **422**, using Long-and-Short Stitch. Angle your stitches slightly outwards as before **(fig. 38)**. You can also scatter stitches of yellow **782** to add a more saturated yellow to the mix **(fig. 39)**.

### The legs

**22.** It's time to stitch those cute legs! Begin with black **310**, using Long-and-Short Stitch **(fig. 40)**. Graduate to brown **3371**, then use yellow **782** to add a single straight stitch across the leg at the top and middle to separate the three segments **(fig. 41)**.

**23.** Finish the ends of the legs using brown **3031** and Straight Stitch. Concentrate on making the stitches that form the ends as small as you can, then overlap with tiny horizontal stitches shown. **(fig. 42)**.

### The abdomen

**24.** Row upon row of tonal shades make embroidering the abdomen a very therapeutic experience.

Using Long-and-Short Stitch, begin with brown **3371**, graduating to yellow **420 (fig. 43)**. Then add brown **801** using a more scattered placement both at the edge of and through **420 (fig. 44)**.

TIP

*Remember, if you're unsure of colour placement, refer to the Colour Guide at the beginning of the project.*

**25.** Continue adding rows of tonal shades to the abdomen using Long-and-Short Stitch. I've broken the rows down into stages, working first through brown 3371 and **801**, then yellow **420** and **782** (**fig. 45**).

**26.** Go back to brown 3371, then **3031** and **801**. Keep angling the outer stitches to add realistic movement to the bee's abdomen (**fig. 46**).

**27.** Carry on with Long-and-Short Stitch to add yellow **420** and **782**. Your stitches will begin to flare out to the sides as the shape broadens, flowing into brown 3371 (**fig. 47**).

**28.** As pictured, add a scattered highlight of yellow **422** using Long-and-Short Stitch to the previous band of yellow **782**. Then add a soft scattering of **3031** to the last embroidered row of brown **3371** (**fig. 48**).

**29.** Still using Long-and-Short Stitch, embroider the final rows, beginning with yellow **420** (**fig. 49**). Add a scattered highlight of **422** as before, then continue with a row of solid brown **3371** and a final row of yellow **420**, again with a scattering of **422** (**fig. 50**). The end of the honey bee's abdomen is stitched in solid **3371** (**fig. 51**).

102

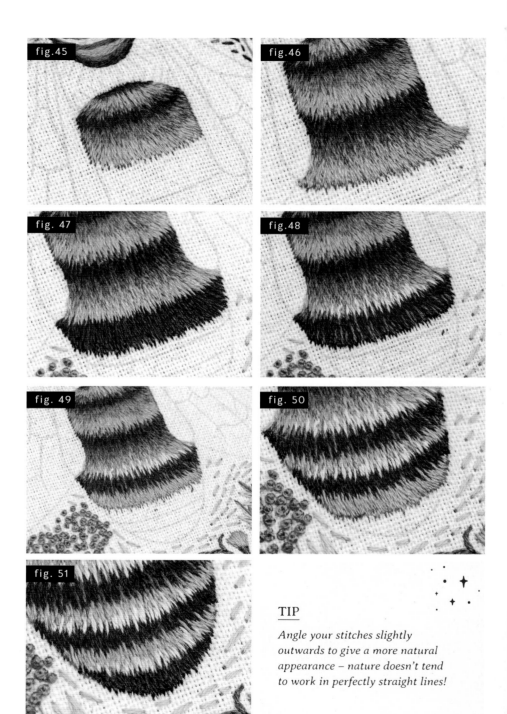

fig.45 fig.46 fig. 47 fig.48 fig. 49 fig. 50 fig. 51

### TIP

*Angle your stitches slightly outwards to give a more natural appearance – nature doesn't tend to work in perfectly straight lines!*

fig. 52

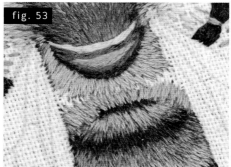

fig. 53

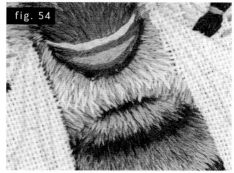

fig. 54

fig.55

**30**. Before we move on to the final stage, let's fill the little fluffy section that connects the thorax to the abdomen. Beginning with brown **801**, create individual Straight Stitches radiating out from the two curved edges to be connected (**fig. 52**). Embroider radiating Long-and-Short Stitch in yellow **402**, following the curves to leave a small triangular gap on both sides (**fig. 53**).

**31**. Finish with yellow **422** to fill in the gaps, scattering it along the edges. Be careful to leave the gaps free to show where the thorax meets the abdomen (**fig. 54**).

### The wings

**32**. We're now at the final stage of the design – the wings. Using one strand of brown **3031**, outline the wings as pictured, using Split Back Stitch. At this point only outline the inner veins, leaving the edges of the wings unstitched (**fig. 55**).

The stitched outline is purely a guide for you to differentiate the different segments of the wing. Therefore, don't worry if this is super tidy or not, as we will be stitching over it at the end.

TIP

*If you notice gaps in the completed abdomen, you can go back and fill some of them in. Don't be afraid to layer your stitches a little as it adds texture and interest to the design.*

Honey Bee

**33**. Using brown **3862**, begin filling in the wings with Long-and-Short Stitch. Then, stitch all the areas on both wings that use **3862** (**fig. 56**). Remember to use the Colour Guide if you are unsure about placement – most of the sections contain two different colours so avoid stitching too far over a segment.

**34**. Now fill in all the areas of the wings that use brown **3863** with Long-and-Short Stitch (**fig. 57**), then repeat with **3864** (**fig. 58**). Refer to the Stitch Direction diagram if you're unsure of which direction your stitches should lie.

**35**. Using Long-and-Short Stitch, fill in the remaining areas of the wings using white **3865** (**fig. 59**). This creates the illusion of light reflecting on the surface, adding a sense of reality and dimension to the embroidery.

**36**. Now that the different segments of the wings have been filled in, it's time to redefine the veins using Split Back Stitch. Starting at the top, use brown **3371**, graduating down the wing, changing to **3031**, then to **801** (**fig. 60**).

You did it! You've finished your honey bee. Feel proud of yourself for your patience and passion. It's nice to take a few moments to soak in your craftsmanship. I hope you enjoyed stitching your little creation.

104

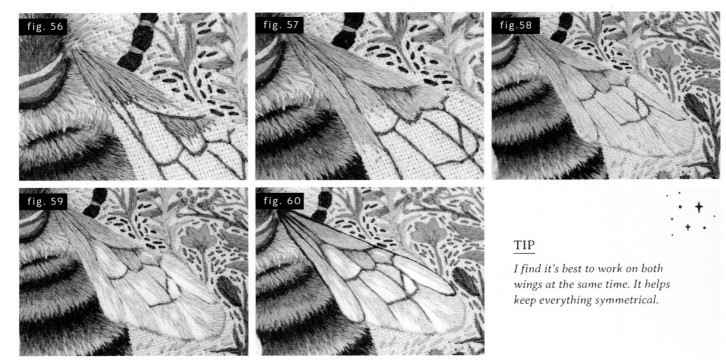

fig. 56  fig. 57  fig.58  fig. 59  fig. 60

### TIP

*I find it's best to work on both wings at the same time. It helps keep everything symmetrical.*

Honey Bee

# HOW TO FINISH

There is a variety of ways to finish and frame your embroidery – my favourite is to keep it in a hoop. I adore the circular shape, which emphasizes that the artwork is hand-embroidered and not painted. When I display my embroidery in a hoop, I always use one of my hand-stained hoops, which I prepare myself.

## PREPARING YOUR HOOP

Varnish the surface of the hoop with a quick-drying wood stain, then allow it to dry for as long as possible before mounting your precious embroidery in it. The benefit of a varnished wood stain is that the varnish remains on the surface of the hoop, forming a protective barrier rather than deeply penetrating the wood. The varnish hardens and won't stain or rub off onto your fabric.

## MOUNT YOUR EMBROIDERY

**1.** Begin by securing your finished embroidery in the hoop in the same way you did before stitching (see Transferring the Patterns, Steps 3 and 4). This time, though, ensure that the screw is positioned exactly at the top of the design.

## TRIM THE EXCESS

**2.** Using sharp scissors, cut away the excess fabric from the embroidery, following the curve of the hoop, to leave a 2.5cm (1in) border (**fig. 1**).

## GATHER THE FABRIC

**3.** Thread your needle with 3–6 strands of embroidery thread (floss) and tie a large knot in the end. You will need no more than 1.5 times the circumference of the hoop.

**4.** Turn the embroidery face down and insert the needle into the excess fabric from the back, to hide the knot. Use Running Stitch around the whole piece, stitching through the excess fabric only, approximately half way between the hoop and the fabric's edge.

**5.** When you are back at the start, push the needle through to the back of the excess fabric. Pull the thread (with the needle still intact) and the fabric will gather neatly together (**fig. 2**).

**6.** Keeping the gathered edge taut, tie a sturdy knot as close to the fabric as possible to keep the tension in place for a flat, even finish. Trim the knot, and you're done!

106

## FINISHING IDEAS

- Choose whichever shade of stain you prefer. Personally I prefer a darker shade as the bold effect frames the embroidery so well. The rich, deep colour connotes more of the medieval or Victorian aesthetic I strive for.

- Tie a piece of ribbon or embroidery thread (floss) around the screw to hang your hoop on the wall.

- If you don't want to mark your wall with a nail, the hoop is so light that I often find hanging with a piece of washi tape will suffice.

- To add your signature to the embroidery, stitch your name and the date onto the back of the fabric before you pull the fabric taut.

- You could also embroider your design onto a cushion, garment, banner, canvas or any other item you wish to experiment with.

### TIP

*I like to use pinking shears to trim the excess fabric as they reduce the chances of fraying.*

How to Finish

## ACKNOWLEDGMENTS

Many thanks and love to all of the magical people that have supported and encouraged me as I pieced together this book.

To everyone at David & Charles, especially Ame Verso and Jenny Fox-Proverbs, for guiding me through the process of creating this book. Your encouraging words and enthusiasm helped me, not to mention your never-ending patience.

To my parents, thank you for giving me the space to be myself growing up, for introducing me to an abundance of wholesome films, music and books. Thank you for raising me in the beautiful British countryside, which has been a continuous source of inspiration for me.

To my sister, Beth, thank you for always bringing out my playful side, for making me laugh and for the daily video calls during all of lock-down whilst I was writing this book.

To my dear friend Mari for being there through the entire process of writing this book – your love and generosity helped me more than you could ever know. Without you, writing this book through lockdown would have never happened.

To my friends I have never met in real life, I am beyond grateful for the community we have created together on Instagram. You have all instilled me with confidence, inspiration and purpose. To everyone who has followed my embroidery journey and encouraged me, you have given me the gift of a free and creative life, and I can't thank you all enough.

## ABOUT THE AUTHOR

Emillie Ferris is an embroidery artist based in rural Warwickshire, UK. After moving to a city for university, she realized she missed the countryside and its slower pace of life. It was from there in 2013 that she began her embroidery journey. Emillie sells her tutorials, kits and original artworks on Etsy with the help of her growing Instagram community. She has been featured on numerous websites, including This is colossal, Design*sponge and Frankie as well as being featured in magazines such as *Vogue Brazil* and *Town & Country* magazine. Emillie's work, although mostly fuelled by her passion for needlecraft, draws inspiration from wildlife, slow-living, natural history, folklore and the British countryside. When she's not creating, Emillie makes a point to savour all moments that make her feel alive, and is particularly fond of wild swimming, dancing, playing the ukulele, cooking with friends and cycling along the canal during golden hour.

You can follow more of Emillie's journey through her Instagram account @emillieferris and on her website www.emillie-ferris.co.uk.

## SUPPLIERS

These are a few of the suppliers I use for my basic tools and materials:

**WWW.WOOLWAREHOUSE.CO.UK**
DMC embroidery thread (floss)
Kona Cotton

**WWW.DMC.COM**
DMC embroidery thread (floss)

**WWW.JJNEEDLES.COM**
John James needles

## INDEX

109

A DAVID AND CHARLES BOOK
© David and Charles, Ltd 2022

David and Charles is an imprint of David and Charles, Ltd
Suite A, Tourism House, Pynes Hill, Exeter, EX2 5WS

Text and Designs © Emillie Ferris 2022
Layout and Photography © David and Charles, Ltd 2022

First published in the UK and USA in 2022

ISBN-13: 9781446308486 hardback
ISBN-13: 9781446380161 EPUB
ISBN-13: 9781446380154 PDF

This book has been printed on paper from approved suppliers and
made from pulp from sustainable sources.

Printed in China through Asia Pacific Offset for:
David and Charles, Ltd
Suite A, Tourism House, Pynes Hill, Exeter, EX2 5WS

10 9 8 7 6 5

Publishing Director: Ame Verso
Editor: Jessica Cropper
Project Editor: Jenny Fox-Proverbs
Designer: Sam Staddon
Pre-press Designer: Ali Stark
Illustrations and Photography: Emillie Ferris
Production Manager: Beverley Richardson

David and Charles publishes high-quality books on a wide range of
subjects. For more information visit www.davidandcharles.com.

Share your makes with us on social media using #dandcbooks and
follow us on Facebook and Instagram by searching for @dandcbooks.

Layout of the digital edition of this book may vary depending on
reader hardware and display settings.

# THE TRANSFERS

To get you stitching straight away, the iron-on transfers allow
you to press the template directly on to your fabric, ready for the
outline and filling stitches shown in the book. Tear your chosen
design carefully along the handy perforated line, then turn to
Transferring the Templates for easy-to-follow steps and advice.

DANDELION

# SUNFLOWER (WITH BACKGROUND)

# SUNFLOWER (WITHOUT BACKGROUND)

# MUSHROOM

ROBIN (WITH BACKGROUND)

# ROBIN (WITHOUT BACKGROUND)

HONEY BEE (WITHOUT BACKGROUND)

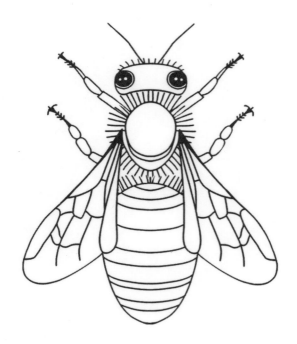